Selling by Telephone

Selling by Telephone

*Tested Techniques to Make
Every Call Count*

Len Rogers

Kogan
Page

Copyright © LA Rogers 1986

First published in Great Britain in 1986 by
Kogan Page Ltd, 120 Pentonville Road, London N1 9JN

British Library Cataloguing in Publication Data
Rogers, Len
Selling by telephone
1. Telephone selling
I. Title
658.8'12   HF5438.3

ISBN 1-85091-186-X
ISBN 1-85091-187-8 Pbk

Typeset by V & M Graphics Ltd, Aylesbury, Bucks
Printed in Great Britain by
Billing & Sons Ltd, Worcester

Contents

Introduction

Selling on the telephone is an art that has to be learned, practised and continuously developed in line with your business.

Advantages of telephone selling

The telephone can get action fast. Prospects will have immediate information about your product or service, and what it can do for them. Ideas can be formulated quickly. Selling is speedier because there is no sitting back taking tea or coffee with the prospect. You have to get to the point without delay. The most effective way of getting ideas to the largest number of prospects in the shortest possible time is by telephone. If there are only two real live prospects in twenty possibles, they can soon be sorted out by phone. You need not spend hours travelling, parking, and waiting until it is convenient to talk.

The telephone keeps you busy. Personal selling day-by-day, driving, walking, waiting, more waiting, chatting, then face-to-face selling has one great drawback: inertia. It is difficult to get started. You sit making plans, thinking how good it is going to be and, by the time you are ready to start, it is time for lunch.

The phone helps to eliminate inertia – you simply pick up the receiver, dial, or press buttons. You will be so busy getting new numbers and telling your story, you will not have time to get discouraged.

The right approach to telephone selling

Whenever you attempt to sell by telephone you are faced simultaneously with an advantage and disadvantage. Once you are through to your client you can talk directly, without interference, because the telephone takes precedence over everything and everyone else in the room. But you can only hear the person. You cannot see the face, the expressions, nor observe the 'body-language'. Neither can your correspondent: you are just a voice. If you have never met you are as big (or small) as the personality you project.

When using the telephone you must employ the right language, words, the appropriate tone of voice. You may not be able to sell something concrete on the telephone, but you can sell your company, your product, your service, yourself. You can create images and sell them. Always talk in the language of the listener if you can, meaning that words and phrases employed should be those used by the person at the other end of the phone. Think of the vocabulary of the computer world – hardware, software, ROMs, RAMs, bytes, floppies, winchesters, 32-bit precision, CAD/CAM systems, or of the publishing world – back-ends, front ends, spine brass (!), half-tone, squared-up, drop, raise, 24-up, 32-up, offset, set-off; it fair takes your breath away. When you talk to the person at the other end of the phone, think of the environment in which he or she is located. Try to imagine the surroundings. Your conversation will then be just that bit more related to the listener's situation.

Styles of telephone conversation

Here is a travel agent talking on the phone with someone who is thinking of taking a late holiday in India:

Customer: We were thinking about a package tour to India. Do you have any?

Agent: When were you thinking of going?

Customer: Late-ish September.

Agent: Well, madam, we have a number of packages. For example, we have an excellent five-day tour based in Kashmir from £250. A chance for you to see the magnificent mountain peaks, lush green fields and trees, cascading waterfalls. You would stay in the capital city of Srinagar with its old wooden houses and bridges; be able to visit the fabulous bazaars in the narrow streets, see wood carvers, silk ...

This is not the language of telephone selling; it is the language of the travel brochure. However interesting and informative the words might be, you expect to read such things, not hear them. The agent skilled in telephone selling would probably say something like this:

Agent: Well, madam, you have the choice of any number of attractive tours. How long a trip are you thinking of?

Customer: Oh, a fortnight or so.

Agent: And would it be just for you, madam?

Customer: No. My husband as well.

Agent: I see. Now the climate varies considerably from one part of the country to another during the year. Late September and October you'd be all right in say, Kathmandu, which is nice all year round. That's in Nepal, of course. I'll put some brochures in the post and mark what I think you should consider. Then I'll phone you in a couple of days and see what you think. May I have your address please?

That's selling. No order has been obtained. No money has been promised. No appointment agreed. Just straightforward selling of the service offered by the agent. You can hear that the agent's response needs developing. The first sentence about climate can be improved. As it is, it does not create an image that links the prospective customer with the agent. Better would be:

Agent: India has a very wide range of climates through the year. One or other of our staff has been to all the places in the brochures. I went to Kashmir last year myself. In late September you'll be better in some areas than others, and you don't want to spend your holiday in the rain; there are so many marvellous things to see. I'll put some brochures in the post, mark what I think you should consider, then phone you in a couple of days and I, or someone here, will be able to tell you more about where you fancy going.

In Chapter 1 you will find another variation on this theme.

What you need when telephoning

Before picking up the phone to make a call, make sure you have something handy with which to write, to write on, a diary, and full information on the product or service you are going to talk about. Simple spiral-bound notebooks with a line down the right- hand side, providing a 3 cm margin, are useful. Here you can note down the content of conversations you have had, telephone numbers, addresses, dates, and so on. Never tear out a page; keep the notebooks as part of a permanent record. Have a clock or watch near the telephone, rather than on your wrist, so as to leave both hands free. A second timepiece showing the current time in the country you are contacting is also useful. After all, if you are telephoning at noon, your correspondent in Italy will have gone to lunch, and if you phone much later than that, your contact in Bombay will already have gone home. In this book are ideas, suggestions, dialogue examples, outlines of problems and information on how to solve them. It covers the whole spectrum of the interesting phenomenon of selling by telephone, more popular and important today than ever before in this technological world, where speed is of the essence. Think about the skills and techniques explained here, adapt them to your own situation and practise them on your next telephone call. As soon as you find something you can use to your advantage, adopt it into your own sales system.

Opportunities in telephone selling

Telephone selling proves the law of averages. You are not going to sell to everyone you phone, but the number you sell to will be in proportion to the number you call up. Initially it may be 2 per cent. If you phone 200 people, on these figures you will sell to 4 people; if you phone 500 you will be selling to 10 people. As you do more telephone selling you will improve. Your technique will gradually become more skilful because, as with any other activity, practice tends to make perfect. By the time you are phoning the three-hundredth prospect your 'hit' rate will have increased until you find that you are selling to 5 per cent of the people you phone, so when you reach 500 calls, you will have sold to 25 people. You will be told that luck plays a great part in this; when you are really successful in selling by phone, 'You're lucky!' will be a regular comment. Remember that the real meaning of 'luck' is when thorough preparation meets an opportunity. If you want to give yourself a chance of being successful in selling on the phone, be prepared. When you are thoroughly prepared and meet an opportunity, you will have the confidence and knowledge to make a sale.

Chapter 1

The Power of Positive Thinking

Thinking positively will increase your opportunities of succeeding in whatever you attempt. If you can think 'yes' things rather than 'no' things, your general manner (and mannerisms) will be positive rather than negative, enthusiastic rather than depressive, and this will quickly be transmitted to people with whom you talk:

Agent: Mrs Brown?

Customer: Yes?

Agent: I have the information now about your holiday to India. The airline has offered us an excellent deal and we've got a special rate for the hotel you wanted. I feel sure you'll have a wonderful time. I was there myself last year.

There is feeling in the words and voice. It's not just a recital of information. Such a manner does not come without being worked at. You have to assess the situation, make sure you have all the data, believe in your ability, know that you can succeed and then act accordingly. Never be afraid of fantasizing; there is no harm in 'building castles in the air' if you then set about constructing foundations!

But avoid the danger of over-confidence, of 'big-headedness'. The man who never entertains the idea that his positive thoughts might fail to come to fruition is inflexible, unable to adapt to the changing world. Positive thinking is not simply latching on to one set of beliefs and ignoring the possibility of anything else. It means always looking for plus points in any situation and developing them: a skill that can be acquired. Look for good everywhere. When you meet obstacles, work to transform them into stepping stones.

Coping with an unsuccessful deal

You have planned to sell someone a particular product and, as soon as you open the phone conversation, you learn that he has already placed the order with another company:

You: Good afternoon. This is James of Blackburn Electronics. May I speak with Mr Tudor please?

Secretary: Just a moment, Mr James; putting you through.

Tudor: Hullo, Mr James. What can I do for you?

You: Ah! Mr Tudor, I've got some updated figures on the resistance tests we've conducted on your proposed new ...

Tudor: [Interrupting] Oh! Mr James, I'm sorry. We've decided to instal the alternative equipment. We were very impressed with yours of course. It wasn't price; you're both about the same. But, as the other company were pressing and had the equipment more or less ready, we decided to go ahead with them and not worry too much about the extra performance. I think you understand.

You: Yes, Mr Tudor. Of course I do. I'll look in on you when I'm in your area later in the year.

Tudor: OK, Mr James. Look forward to that. Goodbye.

Any time you then spend thinking about your 'loss' is negative.

Other opportunities

Instead, immediately you realize that you are not going to get the order, try considering the future. If this is a type of order that will not be repeated, in other words, a one-off, you must think of other opportunities open to you. There are more one-off orders to search for, more prospective buyers to find. What lessons can be learned from this present situation? How can these provide you with advantages in future negotiations? Are there similar possible customers you can call on? Can you strengthen your sales presentation? Do you really know why the order went to the other supplier? If the real reason was lower price, is this true? Is there an initial price with additional costs of operating? Of maintaining? Is it possible to bring out more strongly the benefits of your product that offset your higher price if it is higher? How can these best be put over to a prospective buyer? Do you need to revise your sales presentation? Where do you intend to make your next call? What objectives are you going to set yourself?

This is positive thinking – being adaptable, searching for advantages, for better methods next time, seeing how you can improve so as to take advantage of subsequent opportunities. Getting lucky! Remember that 'luck' is when preparation meets an opportunity.

How to attract interest

You must make your conversation stimulating, deal easily with objections and induce your contact to take the action you want. Make him ready to listen to you. Get the preliminaries over as quickly, but as clearly as you can; don't rush it, but don't dally. This requires you to practise opening gambits. Suppose you, Johnson, are selling an energy-saving device:

Johnson: Good morning, Mr Smith. My name's Johnson of Jones Brothers, Blackburn. I understand you use electrical heating in your machine shops. Is that correct?

Smith: Yes, we do. Why?

Johnson: Mr Smith, would a 1 per cent saving in fuel be of interest to you?

We shall be looking at opening conversations later (see Chapter 4) but remember that you should never quote or use figures that you cannot substantiate. For example, never say:

Johnson: Mr Smith, I can show you how to make a 1 per cent saving on your fuel bill.

Mr Smith might well respond by saying:

Smith: How interesting, Mr Johnson. Just exactly what would that mean then in money terms?

Johnson: Well, I – er – don't know what your fuel bill is but ...

Exit Mr Johnson!

You do not have to be aggressive. You need not shout into the phone. You can make a positive statement in your normal conversational voice.

To get the person on the end of the phone interested in your presentation you should try to engage their attention. Be friendly. Sooner or later you may detect a receptive area. This is where the person expresses a willingness to explore the points you have made further. It may be in the form of a question, a request for you to repeat the point, perhaps asking for a more detailed explanation.

Another area where you must always be positive is in your attitude towards objections. These are inevitable. The person will always say it is inconvenient; the buyer will say that your price is too high; everything is always difficult, different, too late, too big, not enough. You must either overcome the objection immediately it is raised or say that you will deal with it in a moment. Never feel that because the other person raises objections, you are going to lose the sale (see Chapter 9).

Prospect: I suppose you're trying to sell me something.

You: No, sir. I'm hoping to help you to buy something. I wouldn't dream of trying to sell you something you don't need.

Prospect: Well, I think we are all right at the moment. We don't need any more of that line.

You: Is that because you have low sales of them, sir?

No argument; no aggression; no surprise. You have expected him to respond in this way. You have continued with a positive response in the form of a question. We shall go into this selling development in greater detail in Chapter 5.

Positive action and persistence

Induce the prospect to take the action you desire. The positive way to achieve this is to take it for granted that he will do so. You don't ask:

You: Would it be convenient for you to see me next week then?

You assume that the person will see you and you say:

You: Well, let's meet when convenient and tell me, do you prefer a morning or an afternoon?

Being positive also means being persistent. You must keep going. You must call on every prospect to whom you think you can sell. 'Luck' is always on the side of the person who acts.

Self-examination questions on Chapter 1

1/1   What exactly is 'positive thinking'?

1/2   What should you do if you fail to get the order you were expecting when you phoned the prospect?

1/3   What can you do to persuade people to listen to you on the phone?

1/4   What do you need to be 'lucky'?

Chapter 2

How to Make Appointments

You must learn how to organize your time because, as you become skilled at telephone selling, you will find it easy to make appointments, and you don't want to get into the position of not being able to service all your calls properly. An appointment is a means to an end. You have to visit the prospect, make your presentation, draft a report and follow it up.

Whenever you talk with a prospect, ensure that he knows early in the conversation that you are selling. The earlier in your presentation that the listener knows this, the less this will be an obstacle later on. If you try to develop a sales presentation by subterfuge – not letting the listener know that you are selling – then the moment that you do disclose this, it is a first-class reason for the prospect to say 'no, thank you'.

You may have been on the receiving end when this ploy has been used. A poor salesman secures your interest with the pretence that he is conducting a survey. He asks you all sorts of questions and then gives you the opportunity of obtaining a special edition of his product because it is in the interests of a market survey. You suddenly realize that he is selling and you say no! However, if you reveal this early on, you have conditioned the prospect and it cannot subsequently be used as an excuse to say no. Also, early disclosure means that you have to be much more professional in your presentation.

But remember that no one really ever sells anything to anyone. It is the buyer who buys. The real secret of salesmanship is helping the buyer to buy. Make it easy for the buyer to come to a decision to buy from you. Therefore, keep your presentation simple. Don't confuse issues. Make suggestions that are easily distinguished: black, cream or white; red or blue; today, tomorrow or next week; morning or afternoon; two metres or five metres; hard, medium or soft; dry, sweet or demi-sec; high or low, and so on.

Here's a check list of the things you should have before you pick up the phone to make a call:

Report form or pad

At least two writing instruments (they run out of ink, and leads break!)

Diary open at the current week or date

Timepiece

File or correspondence relating to the prospect (if appropriate).

Do not assume that you are going to speak to the prospect directly. You will talk to the telephone operator and then probably the prospect's secretary. Consider that both the operator and the secretary have a task to filter all calls to the prospect. If they didn't, the prospect would spend most of the working day on the phone! Do not use a trick to get through to a prospect. You might succeed. Once! How much better for you and the prospect if he or she knows you are selling and that you are proud and enthusiastic to be doing so.

Importance of selling

Companies stay in business because they are selling products and services to customers. All the production, research, administration, all the management and supervision done inside the company costs money. It is only when you go outside a company and find customers that you make money.

A lot of what is called selling is poorly done, and because of this, selling has a less than splendid reputation. You have built-in problems to overcome. So consider yourself a real salesperson. The fact that you are taking the trouble to study this book means that you are really interested in the process of selling, especially by telephone.

When you call a known customer, even if they have not bought from you for some time, you are a supplier. So when faced with the 'filters' whose job it is to screen calls, you do not need to say that you are selling because you are already one of the company's suppliers. And, in the mind of the filters, suppliers aren't selling!

The correct manner

There is a book on telephone selling which advises sales people to say to the operator, 'Please tell Mr Brown, your financial director, that James White is on the line for him'. Can you imagine anything so self-important and pompous?

'James White of where, sir?' the filter would respond. Unless the operator knows who White is, she or he is not going to win promotion and pay rises by putting through to the financial director anybody who phones in this manner. Consider what could happen:

Caller: Good morning. Will you tell Mr Brown that James White is on the phone for him, please?

Operator: Yes, sir. [phoning internally] Mr Brown, there's a Mr James White on the phone for you, it's personal, I think.

Mr Brown: OK. Put him through.

He's got the interview. Excellent! Or is it? Later ...

Mr Brown: [internal phone to operator] Betty! That was a salesman. It wasn't personal at all. Don't put any more through like that, please.

Operator: Sorry, Mr Brown. He sounded as though he knew you.

The next time you make the call, you cannot try any other ruse to get on to the financial director.

How to get through

So how can we get through to people who, on the surface, do not wish to talk to us? And it must be on the surface because their jobs depend on the amount of work they engender outside the company. Buyers especially have to be aware of what is going on in the market. They are expected to buy from the keenest suppliers. How can they know this adequately if they don't at least talk to people like you?

Let's go back to White's attempt to get through to Brown, the financial director. We must assume that he has a perfectly good reason for wanting to talk to Brown. He has a story to tell; he has a proposition that will be to Brown's advantage:

White: Good morning. I'd like to speak with Mr Brown, please. Your financial director. By the way, may I ask what are his initials?

Operator: Hm! A moment ... R. G., Robert, George.

White: Is it possible to speak with him?

Operator: Who are you, sir?

White: I'm with ABC Financial Group. I'm the area manager.

Operator: Yes, sir. Just a moment. I'll put you through.

	(on internal phone to Brown's secretary) Joan, I've got a chap on the phone, I think he's a salesman. Wants to talk to Robert. Will you deal with him?
Joan:	Yes, Betty, put him through. ... Hullo, Mr Brown's office.
White:	Ah! Good morning. I'd like to have a word with Mr Brown, please, if he's in.
Joan:	He's in, but he's a little busy right now. May I ask what it is? I'm his secretary.
White:	Yes. I'm the area manager of the ABC Financial Group.
Joan:	And what's the nature of your call?
White:	We have a new combined investment project with an inflation-proof assurance scheme that operates on a variable pay-back contribution basis [or some equally abstruse technical description].
Joan:	(not understanding what it is, calls Brown on the internal phone) I've got a chap on the phone, name of White. He's with the ABC Financial Group. I think he's trying to sell you something.
Brown:	Hm! Tell him to write me. Thanks.
Joan:	(to White) Mr White, I've tried to get hold of him but his light's on. I know he's got an important meeting this morning and cannot be interrupted. Will you put the details in the post please? I will see that he gets it.

Here is a better way – a more professional way:

White:	Hullo. Good morning. My name is White, of ABC Financial Group. I want to try to arrange to see Mr Brown, your financial director. Could you tell me first of all, please, what are his initials?
Operator:	Certainly, sir. Just a minute...(pause)...hullo, sir, it's R. G., Robert G. Brown.
White:	Thank you. Now would it be possible to have a word with his secretary?
Operator:	I'll see, sir. Hold the line please. (phoning internally) Joan. There's a Mr White on the phone. He wants to make an appointment with Robert. Will you take him?
Joan:	(Brown's secretary) Yes, Betty ... put him on. (to White) Good morning, Mr White. Can I help you?
White:	Yes. I hope so. I would very much like to make an appointment with Mr Brown to explain an investment proposition to him. I am with the ABC Financial Group. It isn't something that I can put in the post because there are so

many variables. Do you think you could find me about 20 minutes one day next week?

Use the filters

Here's the secret of getting appointments with people who have efficient and effective filters. Use them. Make friends with the filters, the operators, the secretaries, and be completely honest. Make them feel confident that they are not going to be criticized by their bosses for letting you through the screen. They are employed and paid to be secretaries. They are not employed to assess the merits of the propositions that their bosses are paid for. They are expected to be effective as well as efficient. They gradually get to know a lot about the work of their boss. They often make judgements. But whenever they are in doubt, they will pass it to the boss to decide. Therefore, tell them honestly what you are trying to do and don't give them a lot of oblique chatter in an attempt to confuse them and so let you slip through the screen. Leave them in no doubt that your company has a proposition that their boss would not wish to miss, or to be unaware of. I am often asked to see callers in my various activities. I tend to ignore all the facade and smokescreens that many so-called sales people put up in front of me. I have a question that I frequently put to strangers: 'Are you buying or selling?'

If they say 'buying', which I must admit, is very, very seldom, I say: 'Fine! Now, how can I help you?'

If they admit 'selling', I say: 'Fair enough. You have a couple of minutes to tell me what it's all about.'

If, as happens on occasions, people get to see me without an appointment, I am very 'anti' whatever they are selling. It has to be a very good, professional opening to engage my attention. For example, a representative of a wine-bottler once called at a very inopportune moment:

> 'I'm sorry', he said, 'I tried to get you on the phone but couldn't. I've got a few specials on offer. I know you like the particular wine and I didn't want you to think I'd not given you the chance to say 'no'.

How could I refuse to see him!

Getting the appointment

Getting an appointment is only part of the whole process of selling, but it is important. You may have to sell to a committee. Certainly, with highly technical products you have to sell to more than one person. A ploy you can sometimes use is to tell the prospect on the phone: 'I will be in your area next Tuesday [or whenever] and as I'm not there very often, would it be convenient to call?'

The fact that you are making a special journey is beside the point.

I know of a company that sells very complex, costly computer-aided design and manufacturing systems. Each order takes about six months to a year and more to secure. Every prospect is progressed through a number of stages up to the signing of the contract that has to be approved by the board of directors. There's no way they could sell their systems on the phone. But they can certainly use the phone to get appointments and a lot of information before making the personal call. They could also use the phone to follow up the progress of quotations made to prospective customers.

They were progressing an order worth about half a million pounds with a company and it was 'touch and go' as to whether they or their strongest competitor would get the order, although they did have a slight 'edge' as the prospective customer's production director had worked with, and knew, their system. However, both companies' systems were equally sound and cost-effective.

The managing director (call him 'Samson') of this particular company had never met the general manager (call him 'Bright') of the prospective customer. You might consider this unusual but it is often the case. It was suggested that such a meeting might be just the thing to tip the balance in their favour.

Bright was located about 1200 km away from Samson's base. He couldn't simply ring up and offer to travel nearly 2500 km just to have a chat! But, supposing Samson phoned the general manager and said: 'Mr Bright, I will be in your area shortly – I have some business there. As I'm so close, I'd like to look in and see you. When are you free? What about next week?'

As far as Bright was concerned, Samson did not make a special journey but, in fact, he did. And it was well worthwhile because the two of them got on very well together, especially during the evening they spent socially. The general manager's vote was for Samson's company, who eventually won the order.

Being professional

Once, when I called on a large company without making an appointment, the receptionist spoke with the buyer who told her to tell me to phone for an appointment. I thanked her, got into my car, drove away and stopped at the nearest phone box. I asked to be put through to the buyer's department, got his secretary and told her that Mr Giles had asked me to phone for an appointment and ... she put me through to him straight away:

Me: Hullo, Mr Giles. You asked me to phone for an appointment.

Giles: But you only just called in here a few minutes ago.

Me: That's right, sir, and you passed a message to the receptionist for me to phone you for an appointment. So here I am, phoning to see when I may call to see you!

He laughed at my persistence and asked me how far away I was from his office. As I was still quite near, he told me to come back and he would see me.

You must know something about your prospect's business. You must know the products or services they sell. When phoning for an appointment, it must be a step towards the normal selling process. It is a means to an end and not the end itself.

Don't be afraid of asking questions. Frequently, when phoning prospective customers you will hear the words, 'Sorry, but not interested.' A prospect who is not interested has made up her or his mind before possessing the facts. That's not good sense. Change your tactics. Say you are trying to get information about the prospect's company and its products. Ask if the prospect can spare a few minutes on the phone to tell you about their products. Ask questions; learn about their problems. Then, armed with this knowledge, you can study the situation and work out an approach that is based on your knowledge. Your approach is bound to be enthusiastic because you have taken the trouble to think about the customer's situation. But don't stop there. Develop your knowledge about the whole of the industry in which you are working, its production methods, business structure, markets, competitors, commercial procedures and personalities. Then 'set fire' to it. Enthusiasm is knowledge on fire.

When all else fails in trying to get an appointment, you could say: 'Mr Prospect, the success of your company depends on the amount of products you sell. I'm trying to do my bit for my company. Just think how difficult it would be for you if your sales people could never get to see the buyer!'

Self-examination questions on Chapter 2

2/1   Should you let the respondent know that you are selling or try to gain her or his confidence before she or he realizes this?

2/2 Why is cold canvassing sometimes more difficult with personal visits?

2/3 What is the most professional way to make more appointments?

Chapter 3

How to Structure a Telephone Call

Selling by telephone is much the same as selling in any other situation insofar as you must have a definite structure, that is, a structure of sales presentation. It is no use calling on a prospective customer without having a general idea of what to talk about, something to say to the prospect, perhaps even a specific objective.

If your contact is a complete stranger, you will have to use an approach that is markedly different from that to someone you have previously met.

Phoning a stranger

Get to the point quickly, but, if you present it in too blunt or too forceful a manner, you will probably frighten off the prospect before you can put your proposition:

You: Good morning, Mr Prospect. I sell life insurance. Your family's future can be guaranteed, should you die prematurely, for a payment of about £5,000.

Thank you, but no!

You: Is that Mrs Jones?... fine. Good afternoon, Mrs Jones. My name's Finlay of Hitech Fireplaces. Mrs Jones, I believe you have open fires in your house, is that right?... Well, we have an entirely new grate that increases the efficiency of fuel burning by as much as 25 per cent. Would it be possible to call and see you?

Thank you, but no!

You: Hullo, Mr Stewart. This is MacGregor Electronics here. We've got a new control device that's absolutely ideal for your production process. I'd like to call and tell you more about it. ...

Thank you, but no!

You: Mr Prospect, suppose I could tell you how you could make at the very least another 10 per cent profit with your product, would you be interested?

Thank you, but no!

We're not doing too well, are we? We are getting to the point too soon; we are hitting the prospect much too quickly. We haven't even found out if they have the time to talk on the phone. It also happens socially:

You:	Hullo, John. How are you?
John:	Oh! Fine. And you?
You:	Yes. Top form. Tell me, John – er – have you read that article yet? I sent it the other day. ...
John:	Sorry, but we're just sitting down to dinner. Could I call you back later this evening?

Phoning a friend

If you phone a relative, friend or colleague when they may be doing something, you will probably make sure they have the time to talk and are not sitting at a meal, playing cards, standing on a ladder painting, talking with someone else, answering the door to a visitor, just about to go out of the house, or engaged in any of those activities that are more important or urgent than talking with you. Always preface phone conversations in this way:

You:	Hullo! Are you free to talk or are you doing something?

Imagine a similar situation in another setting. You enter a room and are received by your host; you are introduced to two or three people who are standing talking together, drinks in their hands, smiling:

Host:	Ah! I don't think you've met Nigel before have you? Nigel, this is ...
You:	Hullo. Gosh! What a journey I've had. D'you know that stretch between Reigate and Wisley? It was supposed to be open last week. I've never had such a long, fatiguing journey. ...

Thank you, but no!

They don't want to know about your journey. They were talking together. You've interrupted them. They will smile and listen but only out of politeness.

Wait until after the introductions and make sure they want to listen to you. You have to be accepted by them and, if they haven't been talking about something far more interesting or important than car journeys, sooner or later they will ask you polite questions such as: 'What line of business are you in, Nigel?', 'Have you had your holidays yet?', 'Have you come far, Nigel?' Then you can bore them with your journey!

So, 'play yourself in' but remember that if you fail to get to the point in a reasonably short space of time, the prospect is going to wonder just why you are phoning. One of the most unnerving questions you can be asked is, 'What is the point you are making?' or even worse, 'What is the point you are trying to make?'

The structure

Think of any of those ordinary things we do such as making a cake, decorating a room, cleaning the car, replacing an electric plug, going on holiday, taking the children to school or any of the hundred-and-one other activities which we carry out from time to time. There is always a procedure to be followed that makes it easier to complete the task. There are numerous guides and mnemonics around which can help us to remember the order in which things have to be done. Perhaps the oldest one is AIDA, which is used for selling. It stands for Attention, Interest, Desire, and Action. First get the prospect's attention. Then you develop his or her interest in your proposition, create a desire to possess your product and, finally, achieve action.

One that I devised many years ago in my early motoring days is POWER. When visiting the garage for fuel I always thought of this mnemonic. It stands for Petrol, Oil, Water, Electricity (the battery fluid), Rubber (tyre pressure). Even today, I remember to check the other four items when getting fuel for my car but I do not consciously think of the mnemonic.

I have since adapted POWER, for managing. It stands for Plan, Organize, Watch, Evaluate, and Revise. If you want to be a good manager, first you devise your plan, then you set up the appropriate organization to implement it, maintain a 'watching brief' over activities, evaluate the results continuously, and revise as necessary.

Mnemonic plan for telephone selling

Here is a framework for telephone selling into which any telesales proposition can be inserted. It is based on the mnemonic ONROAD:

- Opening
- Need
- Resolution
- Offer
- Assessment
- Decision.

Opening
All selling processes, whether in a face-to-face situation or on the telephone, have to have an opening in which it should be attempted to involve the prospect from the start.

Need
Fundamental to all selling processes because without it there can be no sale.

Resolution
When the real need has been identified then both salesperson and prospect can set about satisfying it.

Offer
Once any obstacles preventing resolution have been made known and understood, the salesperson can make the offer.

Assessment
The product or service offered must be assessed by both prospect and salesperson in relation to the need that has been established.

Decision
This is simply whether or not the prospect is going to do business with the salesperson. It must be implemented by definite action such as giving an order, asking for a quotation, or making a statement of intent to take the matter further.

Any course on salesmanship will doubtless possess its own plan of action and often its own mnemonic to make selling easy. Beware! Selling is *not* easy. It does not conform to a pattern or an array of techniques where all you have to do is to use the plan and success will follow. Any plan of action, pattern of approach, mnemonic, is only an *aid to selling*.

You will have to decide very quickly in the preliminary discussions with the prospect whether you need to go through the total ONROAD sequence or not. Consider:

Salesman: Good afternoon, Mr Prospect. My name's Dungate of Medway Controls. I thought ...

Customer: Oh! I'm so glad you've called. We're short of some 40 mm and 25 mm reducers. Have you got any in stock at Rochester?

Only a fool would start to go through the whole sequence after getting this response from the customer. Already we are in the resolution stage and it is up to Dungate to make the offer.

Self-examination questions on Chapter 3

3/1   Why is it important to have a structure when selling on the telephone?

3/2   Is it necessary to get to the point early in the phone call?

3/3   When making a sales presentation to a prospect, when do you make the offer?

Chapter 4

Opening the Call with a Statement

There are only two ways you can open a sales presentation, whether you're face to face with the customer or on the phone: with a statement or with a question.

On the phone you must be much more careful with the opening as your prospect can only hear you and, if the two of you have never met, what you say and how you say it is the only means of communication. If you were sitting face to face with the prospect, any slight aberration or faltering in your opening might be retrieved by other communicative means – gestures, a smile, body attitude, illustrated literature etc.

Plausibility

Your initial statement must be very carefully constructed to present some characteristic or benefit of your product to the prospect. And this must be believable.

You may have something to offer which can give great benefit to its owner or user, but it may be that the real value of the product can only be appreciated when it is in use.

If so, you have a difficult task in composing your opening remarks convincingly.

A poor opening

Here is an example of how not to open a telephone sale with a statement:

Salesman: Mr Roberts?

Customer: Yes.

Salesman: Good morning, Mr Roberts. I can show you a method of cutting costs in your ...

Customer: [angrily] Who is this?

Not a very good opening. In fact, not an opening at all. The salesman didn't even say who he was, who his company was, or find out whether it was convenient to talk. Straight into the sales talk! He didn't know whether Roberts was the right person, or whether he could influence the purchase.

All the preambles such as 'Good morning', 'Had your holidays yet?', 'How is business?', etc are not opening statements or questions. Opening the sale starts after you have said your greetings, told the respondent who you are, found out if it's convenient at that time, said whom you are representing, and laid the foundation for the opening.

Importance of a good opening

Consider a speaker who has been invited by an organization to give a talk after a dinner. The meal is coming to a close, coffee has been served, the traditional toast to the monarch made, permission to smoke has been given, the chairman rises, calls for attention, addresses the roomful of people and starts to introduce the speaker. He gives a brief account of the speaker and some of his accomplishments, eventually saying, 'Ladies and gentlemen, it gives me great pleasure this evening to introduce ...'

There is polite applause, the chairman beams at the speaker who gets up, nods thanks to the applause, looks round the room, looks to the side, sees that the chairman is seated and starts.

What he says at that point can intrigue and captivate the audience, or annoy them. He can amuse them or generate hostility; interest or bore them. If he doesn't speak up and project his voice, people at the back of the room may not even know he has started. He has, perhaps, 30 seconds in which to put over his opening remarks to the audience.

When you are face to face with a prospective buyer, you have about the same time to open your sales presentation. On the phone, you probably have less than half this amount of time.

We are not talking about the 'Good morning', 'Good afternoon', 'How is the family?', 'Have you had your holidays yet?', 'Where will you be spending Christmas?', and so on. It is the chairman who introduces the speaker who is, in effect, saying the good mornings; it is the speaker who opens the presentation.

The speaker at a meeting has an advantage over someone talking on the phone. He is unlikely to be cut short. His audience will usually listen with politeness, however much there may be a general desire to get to the bar!

The telephone caller, however, could be interrupted at any time during that crucial 15 seconds or less, which is an additional reason for a really good opening in a telesales presentation.

An opening can only be a statement or a question. You cannot show the product or a picture of the product. The very advantage and priority you have by talking directly with the prospect also means that you cannot waste time with irrelevancies.

Opening with a factual statement

'Mr Prospect, the article on our product in last month's [professional journal] describes it as the leader in its field.'

'The newly designed digital readout on our product gives you instant control over quality.'

'A course of dancing lessons at our academy guarantees success or we refund your payment in full.'

'More fleet operators use our oil than any other brand.'

'The fish we supply to our customers is always fresh and in prime condition because we collect it every day from the boats.'

'The majority of factories use more of our valves than any other make.'

'Companies who have installed our system report savings from around 10 to 40 per cent.'

Of course, such statements must be true, relevant, readily understandable and should arouse interest. These four requirements may be remembered by the mnemonic TRUE:

- True
- Relevant
- Understandable
- Evoke interest.

Opening with a specific topic

Here you link the prospect with a product or service you can provide:

'A couple of weeks ago, I sent you a sample product and said I would contact you to see how it worked out.'

'When we met at the national exhibition, you expressed an interest in our upgraded model. This is now ready and, before arranging a visit, I'd like to check on the maximum flow you think you would need.'

'As I was passing your factory recently I noticed that you appeared to have a problem with ... I have a product which, for a modest outlay, can overcome it.'

'I couldn't help noticing the quantity of waste paper [or whatever] that you throw away. I'd like to tell you briefly how this can be made valuable to you.'

'I saw some of your attractive brochures the other day. I'd like to give you some information that could mean a very acceptable saving on your printing.'

'Your company doubtless has a heavy bill for travelling expenses. I'd like to show you some data on a firm similar in size to yours that has enabled them to reduce their travel costs substantially.'

Third party reference

Before you use this opening, it is essential you establish that the third party is regarded as a reliable reference by the prospect:

'Your Birmingham factory manager has been having very good results with our product and I thought you would like to have details.'

This is useful only if the prospect knows the Birmingham manager and generally approves of him. If he dislikes him, or perhaps detests him, you will learn very quickly how not to win friends and influence people!

If this information cannot be easily obtained, try to find out what the relationship is between the prospect and the reference you are thinking of using, by suitable questions early on. Be prepared to switch your opening, should you discover that the relationship between the prospect and the third party you were thinking of using is less than friendly:

'Mr Prospect, I assume you know John Bell's operation in Birmingham. I saw him recently, mentioned I was contacting you and he passes on his good wishes.'

And you listen very carefully to the reaction to this, especially to the tone of voice. This can often tell you a lot more than the actual words. Of course, you would be wise to check with the referee to see if it would be sensible to use him with the prospect.

You do not necessarily have to have personal references. You can talk about buildings, factories, offices. The criterion is that the prospect must think highly enough of the reference you are using:

'The paint that was used on the XYZ building was our special anti-corrosion product. When you are considering your next repaint you could do worse than consider our special finishes.'

'The cost of heating the *Daily Echo* building has been cut by 75 per cent because they have installed our solar window panels.'

'The managing director's secretary said I should contact you about ...' [you should first of all talk with the MD's secretary, ask for help, and ask for the name of the prospect].

Opening on a minor point

You are selling; the prospect is buying. Buying and selling are simply different views of the same transaction! However, buying is usually a set of major decisions. The decision-making process is very complex and a number of influences affect the decision. Sometimes it is better to open on a minor point.

If you were selling a set of encyclopaedias you should not open with:

'Mr Prospect, the 25 volumes will provide you with all the knowledge of the modern world. The fine, leather bound set will cost you £2,000.'

This is better:

'Mr Prospect the 25 volumes will provide you with all the knowledge of the modern world and you have the right to purchase the special, updating volume each year for only £5 in the same matching binding as your original purchase.'

Opening on a minor point is to prevent hitting the prospect 'between the eyes' with your proposition. You have to find out a lot more about the prospect before you can open with a blunt major statement.

If you were trying to sell a certain system which necessitated selling the prospect the idea that it was worth seeing you to have a look at the system actually working, you could open on a minor point:

'Mr Prospect, while there are many systems available, what I'd like to show you is one that has the lowest annual running cost of all. When would it be possible to give you a demonstration? Have you an hour spare next week?'

If you use a statement to open, treat it as all other important announcements you make on the phone: it has to be constantly reviewed and polished to make it easy to handle, believable and readily understood.

Self-examination questions on Chapter 4

4/1 What are the advantages that an after-dinner speaker has over you as a salesperson on the phone when you are making your opening remarks?

4/2 Why do you need to be more careful with your opening statement on the phone than when face to face?

4/3 When does the opening of the sale actually start?

Chapter 5

Opening the Call with a Question

The question opening is the most useful and, at the same time, the most tricky. If you ask a loosely constructed question you will receive some very difficult, or at least, unhelpful answers. Your questions should be prepared so that they and their answers can be related to your product or service benefits and subsequent well-structured sales presentation.

Whenever you embark on your sales talk you must know where you can go. No sensible motorist will set off into unknown country without some idea which cities, towns and villages are where, without a map, and not knowing whether he has sufficient petrol in the car or if there are adequate petrol stations *en route*.

Because you cannot see the prospect and are unable to show him the product or illustrations, or make use of a presenter or sales aids, you need to control the presentation by what you say and how you say it.

Often the prospect himself will want to direct the conversation; this is understandable. There is no value to be gained in your fighting the prospect and insisting on maintaining control in the face of a determined buyer:

'Look, I'm busy. Write to me about it, please.'

'Sorry. Cut the talk. How much is it?'

'You're trying to sell me something. What is it?'

'I don't want all the sales talk. What are your sizes and prices?'

The secret is to let the prospect take care of the conversation while you control the sales aspect.

The importance of listening

The key to successful telephone presentation is to listen carefully to what the prospect has to say and then use that to lead back into your sales talk:

Customer: Look, I'm busy. Write to me about it, please.

Salesman:	Certainly, Mr Prospect. May I have your initials? Thank you. I'll send you details. They will cover all applications. You would need all applications I assume, or is there a specific task that has to be performed?
Customer:	Sorry. Cut the talk. How much is it?
Salesman:	[quoting lowest price] Fifteen pounds, sir. That includes everything. I take it yours would be a normal application. You wouldn't need a widget sorter would you?
Customer:	You're trying to sell me something. What is it?
Salesman:	The lowest priced solid-state control system on the market, but I'm not trying to sell it, sir. Not unless you have need of it. Is your present quality control system continuously monitored?
Customer:	I don't want all the sales talk. What are your sizes and prices?
Salesman:	Our sizes cover 100 per cent of the needs of the market, sir. Our prices aren't the lowest but you can't buy the same or better quality at our prices. Do you buy solely on price?

Is the customer buying on price?

If he is, and your prices are not the lowest he can get, you do not stand much of a chance of selling to him on the phone. You will have to retreat to fight another day. You will have to get an appointment and develop a personal sales presentation where you can put over the advantages of his buying from you.

However, the prospect who demands to know your prices immediately you open may not be buying on price. For example, a camera can cost as little as £10, or from £500 upwards; price is a useful indication of its capabilities. Test this yourself: visit a camera shop, tell the assistant that you are thinking of buying a camera and listen to the response. Most likely you will be asked what price range you have in mind. If you are conversant with cameras, you will know that when you ask for a camera in a shop by stating that you want one around £100, you are indicating the type of camera you are looking for.

The lesson is clear. Don't assume that because you are asked about price that the prospect is buying on price. He may simply be wanting to know the category of the product you are selling.

Making notes

Note comments on every call you make, with the prospect's name, initials, position in the company, address, phone number, using the recommended spiral notebook (see Introduction), add a brief word or two about topics discussed, and any figures you or the prospect may quote.

If points strike you as you listen, jot them down so that you can use them during and after the call. Use the margin to signal urgent matters, dates to follow up and clearly cross through each section when it has been dealt with. By glancing down the margins, you can quickly establish what matters still have to be tackled or progressed. Enter any follow-ups to be done in your diary.

It is a good idea to make a brief note in particular of the responses you get to specific question openings. By periodically appraising these responses you can polish your opening questions and develop suitable follow-up comments.

Using the question opening

You may find that question openings are difficult to use because of the nature of your product, which may be completely new in concept and hard to explain on the phone. You may be selling an intangible such as advertising space, insurance, consultancy, an inspection service or something with an equal lack of substance and feel at a loss to know how to start, how to open.

To cope with these feelings, remember that no one buys a product for itself alone, but for the satisfaction, benefits or service it provides: we do not buy new golf clubs, we buy lower scores; we don't really rent strips of sand on a beach in the summer, we buy dreams; we don't want 6 mm twist drills, we want 6 mm holes; we don't buy boxes of matches, we buy boxes of flames.

Whatever your product, you must think of its use from the viewpoint of the prospective buyer. You must think about the benefits he will have if your product is acquired, and then construct simple, easy-to-understand statements or questions that will convey those benefits to the mind of the prospect.

Product benefit questions

Here is an example of an opening question that relates to product benefits and is constructed so as to lead into the subsequent presentation:

'Good morning, Mr Prospect. This is John Smith of Allfasteners Limited. May I ask you, when you meet a difficult fastening problem how do you overcome it?'

Consider other openings that might have been used:

'Do you ever meet difficult fastening problems?'
[Answer: Yes, all the time!]

'Do you know our range of fastenings?'
[Answer: Yes. I have your catalogue.]

'What do you do if you meet a difficult fastening problem?'
[Answer: They're all difficult!]

'Have you seen our range of special fastenings for difficult tasks?'
[Answer: We know your range but send me your up-to-date catalogue.]

'When you meet a difficult fastening problem how do you overcome it?' [This is too direct and tends to create a barrier such as, 'What do you want to know for?', 'Why should I tell you?' and begs the general response, 'Why?']

'When you meet a difficult fastening problem, may I ask, how do you overcome it?' [This is the one we started with and is better because it is a request for information. It softens the approach and tends to avoid the general response, 'Why?']

Always test your openings thoroughly. Make sure that, as far as possible, you have a sentence that is easy to say, easy to understand, polite, and involves the listener.

You should be careful of the form, 'When you have a difficult fastening problem do you know what I would do?' because this does not involve the prospect. This should only be used if you are introducing a topic of considerable interest to the prospect and you can continue with a description that will hold his attention.

A good opening is only the beginning of the sales presentation and you must know where you could go after this, which means that you must have one or more possible objectives for the telephone call. For example, if you have the objective of getting an order every time you start a telesales presentation you will fail to achieve this more times than you succeed.

It is better to realize that you will close a sale perhaps once or twice in 10 to 20 calls. This will save you from becoming too discouraged as call after call fails to achieve an order. As you become accustomed to telephone technique and analyse prospects' responses, you will find your strike rate of orders-to-calls will improve (see Introduction).

It might be more realistic to get the prospect to understand that your product offers excellent value for its price and to consider buying from you when supplies are needed. Such an objective will also give you a secondary aim: to establish when to phone again and make sure the prospect appreciates that you will be phoning on that date.

After you have opened the sales presentation and introduced the product and some of its benefits, the next stage is to establish the *need* of the prospect.

Self-examination questions on Chapter 5

5/1   Why is it difficult to open a sale with a question?

5/2   What is suggested as the key to a successful telephone conversation?

5/3   Why should you test your openings thoroughly?

Chapter 6

Identifying Needs – the Closed Question and the Open Probe

If the prospect has no need for your product you are wasting your own time and his by trying to get an appointment, let alone trying to sell over the phone.

Identifying a prospect's needs is difficult enough in face-to-face situations; on the phone, as we know, there are extra handicaps (see Chapter 4). Everything has to be done with the voice (see also Chapter 13).

However, because of the nature of the medium, you are talking directly into the listener's ear and your conversation may be regarded as privileged and protected; it will not normally be overheard by others in the room. You can be a little more direct and ask more pointed questions because they will be private and the listener will not be made self-conscious, as he would if others could also hear your conversation.

Interpreting the conversation

You should assume that a prospect does not necessarily know what he needs. He may say that he wants one thing while actually requiring something quite different. This is particularly true in the high technology field where you may be selling complex technical products for ordinary purposes. The prospect may not be able to put into words what his organization needs and it is up to you to interpret what is being discussed in terms of understandable needs that can be related to products you are able to supply.

Take great care on the phone to help the prospect understand what is really needed. Never talk in a manner that could be misunderstood as being 'superior'; that is, never talk down to the customer. You must concentrate on what the prospect says and how he says it, so that you can establish what is really needed more quickly.

You can best identify needs by asking questions and listening to the answers. But the questions you put to the prospect should be of two kinds:

- Closed questions
- Open probes

Closed questions

These narrow down the conversation to specific points. They can be answered by 'yes', 'no', 'black', 'white', 'two', 'six', 'every week', and so on. They ask for fairly precise responses. Examples are:

'What colour do you use now?'

'Which day do you usually service the machinery?'

'How may locks are there?'

'Have you always used singles?'

'Are you left- or right-handed?'

'Where does this happen?'

'Where is the stock kept now?'

'How many would you need?'

'Do you use any numerical control equipment now?'

All of these questions can be answered by one response. Each one focuses the respondent's reply to a single statement and does not readily invite further discussion.

Open probes

A closed question is used to obtain a clear-cut response and limits the conversation, whereas the open probe seeks more information, opens out the conversation and invites the prospect to expand on what has been said. Examples are:

'Why do you think that happens?'

'In what way?'

'Oh!'

'This is because ...?'

'Would you mind explaining?'

'If you had the opportunity what would you choose?'

'Why is that?'

'Hm!'

'Really?'

'You think so?'

A simple response such as 'Hm!' will work, provided that you show genuine interest in what is being said. The difficulty is that you cannot use a facial expression on the phone to accompany the words. But, and this is an important but, your attitude does communicate over the telephone wires and if you smile, your voice will 'smile'. If you are puzzled and frown, your voice will sound 'puzzled'. It follows that you must really 'live' the part you play on the phone.

Use of question technique

Even though the prospect may dominate the conversation, you can control the sale presentation by a judicious use of closed questions and open probes. If you use these two types of question skilfully, you can direct the conversation into those areas most advantageous to you. While your respondent has the oars and does the rowing, you steer the boat, sometimes subtly with an almost imperceptible alteration of course, at other times by a complete change of direction:

Salesman:	Good afternoon, Mr Peters. My name's Wilson of Scott Services. Do you have a couple of minutes free to talk at the moment? [closed]
Peters:	Yes. Who did you say you are?
Wilson:	Doug Wilson of Scott Services. We operate throughout Scotland and part of England, training middle and upper management. Do you have your own training department, Mr Peters? [closed]
Peters:	No.
Wilson:	But, presumably you do some training; may I ask how many the company employs, sir? [closed]
Peters:	About 1500 on this site; and about half in Dundee. When we want any training we send our people on an appropriate course.
Wilson:	I see, sir. I'd rather not take up too much of your time on the phone now, but I'd like to call and see you. Where is your interest in training? [open]
Peters:	Well everywhere. Across the board.
Wilson:	Really? [open]
Peters:	Yes. But we don't do a great deal at the moment.
Wilson:	I see. I think you may be interested in some of our developments. Would it be convenient to see you this week – I am in the area? [closed]
Peters:	Can't you put something in the post to me?

Wilson:	Certainly, Mr Peters. What exactly would you be interested in? [open]
Peters:	What do you do? I don't know your organization.
Wilson:	We've been in the business of training and supplying special services for about 20 years. Our range of training is very wide. We have over 30 training centres in Scotland alone. I can certainly put one of our brochures in the post to you but as all our training is result-oriented, it will only confirm what I'm telling you now. If you can spare me about half an hour I can provide you with a lot of information that might be useful to you. I will be in your area later on this week. Could I call and see you, say, Thursday or Friday? [closed]
Peters:	This week – let me see; I've a little time on Thursday morning.
Wilson:	That would suit me, Mr Peters. What time will be convenient? [closed]
Peters:	About 11.00?
Wilson:	Fine. I'll be there at 11.00. That's this Thursday, the 14th, 11.00. Look forward to seeing you, Mr Peters.

Note the use of the closed question to focus on getting the appointment. The first time the salesman tries, the customer declines. He then uses an open probe to develop the conversation and another closed question to focus on the appointment. Had he not obtained an appointment, he would continue with open probes to get more information to help him with his presentation.

Never be too discouraged at getting a 'no' from the prospective customer. It is a natural reaction and indicates that the prospect is not yet convinced. You have to 'keep on selling' and do this with open probes and closed questions. Some authorities have suggested that a salesperson should take three 'no' responses before accepting that the prospect really means no. Perhaps we should agree that the first 'no' is probably a natural response and not accept it as genuine. We should continue with our conversation and make use of open probes and suitably focused closed questions to search for the prospect's real needs. Don't forget to listen carefully.

Importance of making notes

Cultivate the habit of jotting down on your pad points made by the prospect in response to your open probes. Points that seem at first unimportant may later become crucial to your discussion. Here is an example of a department store salesman dealing with a customer on the phone:

Customer: I want some curtaining material for my sitting room please. What do you have in stock?

Salesman: Certainly, madam. Do you have any particular colour in mind? [open probe]

Customer: Well the ones I have now are plum-coloured velvet. I'd like a change but I'm not sure about colours. There's quite a lot of red in the carpet. It's a Turkish design.

Salesman: Is it a large room, madam? [closed question]

Customer: Not really. About 40 feet or so by about 25, I suppose.

Salesman: [not listening properly, doesn't jot down the dimensions and only hears 'not really'] What you need then, I think, is a fairly small design. We have some very nice contemporary prints in. From Belgium.

The salesman has put in appropriate open probes but has not listened to the answer about the size of the room. The woman thinks that it is not really a large room but the dimensions would make it quite a large room by ordinary standards. Certainly not a room for curtains with a small design.

The salesman has not had to open the sale. The woman is already in a buying frame of mind. What he does have to do is to search for the real need. And this is where he has come unstuck. The woman's needs are far from clear. He has not even understood the dimensions of the room and so is unable to develop the sale very far. Let us follow the conversation further:

Customer: It sounds a little continental doesn't it? Belgian, you say. Won't the colours fade?

Salesman: Well, not in a soft reddish-brown, which I suggest you need to match the carpet. Blues and purples are difficult, of course, but with the red carpet you wouldn't need these anyway.

Customer: I'm not too sure about the design, though. Contemporary, you say. My house is quite old. I don't think a contemporary design would look right.

Salesman: You would find these would fit in with new or old-fashioned surroundings. You may think they're modern prints, but really they are more stylistic in the conventional, traditional style.

He is in difficulties! Still attempting to sell without finding out what the real need is. 'Old-fashioned' indeed! Perhaps this is a slip of the tongue. And, what does, 'more stylistic in the conventional, traditional style' mean?

Customer:	Do you have anything there similar to the plum-coloured ones I have now? I would come and see it, of course, but I do have a fair way to come.
Salesman:	[remembering that the customer said that she wanted to have a change] But madam, if you want to make a change, I believe you would find these Belgian designs most acceptable. Would it help if I asked our Mr Harris to call and measure up? He can then bring a range of samples?
Customer:	Oh! I don't want anyone to call. Do you have any velveteen material? In plum?

The woman herself has partly disclosed her real need. She doesn't really want a change. She would like to have new curtains in the same expensive material that she has now, but cannot afford it.

Identifying the need

It is so important to find out what the customer really needs before you make any offers. This woman customer is probably thinking of phoning another store now. The sales assistant started well but quickly got out of step, mainly because he did not listen. He didn't even try to find the real needs of the customer. He also had the fixed idea that the room was not very large. If he had jotted down the dimensions and quickly compared them with an 'average' size room, he would have realized that the room was quite large. Probably what the customer needed was a substitute for the curtains she had already, a low-priced curtain material. But the salesman never even explored quality or price.

Remember that there are usually at least two reasons why we do anything – a good reason, and the *real* reason.

Your task when progressing the sale is to find out the real reason – the real need. This may mean that you will have to spell it out for the prospect in terms that he or she will understand. So, you have two objectives when identifying needs: articulating the real need and getting the prospect to understand and agree what this need is.

Self-examination questions on Chapter 6

6/1 Why is the telephone conversation with a listener regarded as privileged?

6/2 What is a closed question?

6/3   What is an open probe?

6/4   Before you make an offer to a prospect, you are advised to achieve something. What is it?

Chapter 7

How to Resolve the Buying Decision

It is essential that, before presenting your sales proposition, you possess a thorough knowledge of the market and competitive products. You should also be fully aware of the current prices, advantages and disadvantages of all the major products in competition with yours.

You use your product knowledge to sell ideas to the prospect. In this way you start the process of resolution of the buying process. You need to know as much as possible about your own product, to answer questions and deal with any objections that may arise. In this way you establish confidence – in your presentation, in your product and in your yourself.

You start by opening the 'selling' part of your telephone conversation and then, as already discussed, you move on to establish the real needs of your prospect and make sure that they are understood. The next stage is for the prospect to make a resolution to satisfy those needs.

Ideally the prospects should satisfy their needs by buying your product or service, but you do not necessarily make a sale on the telephone. You might make sales, of course, if you were phoning customers on a regular basis: a fresh food supplier or a processed food manufacturer contacting hotels and restaurants would find it normal to take orders by telephone.

I used to own a hotel and it was usual for one of our suppliers to phone us on Tuesday mornings to take our order for delivery later in the week. Their telephone sales staff were excellent at finding out what our needs were and offering us special deals on various foods. Because they were skilled in identifying our real needs, they were able to match those needs with attractive offers at equally attractive prices. In short, it was difficult to say 'no'. There was no pressure selling or hard sell. They just found out what our needs were and then made us offers that we could not refuse!

There are many things you cannot sell on the phone in the sense of making your sales presentation and receiving an order. These include highly technical equipment, orders involving substantial sums of money, and products that must be demonstrated to be understood. There would have to be visits, discussion with various people in the organization who are concerned with the purchase, demonstration of your equipment, perhaps a special, customer-oriented demonstration, submission of quotation, negotiation and so on. You cannot sell such a product simply by getting on the phone and talking with a prospective buyer in the company.

Nevertheless, the techniques discussed in this book can be used at any time. Here are two that you can adapt to your own selling situation to make prospects favour your product when resolving to satisfy the specific needs that you have identified and made known to them.

Linking the buying benefits

The first is an almost hypnotic process that seems to attract the prospect to your product. You must first list the attributes of your product or service and determine which of these can be used as buying benefits. Certain attributes are of greater benefit to some people and organizations than to others. Therefore it is vital that you list them and translate them into observable and understandable product benefits. Ask yourself: in what way can this attribute be a benefit to the user?

Some years ago I was handling the marketing for a large company, one of whose factories made carpet sweepers. These are pushed across the carpet on their rubber wheels that revolve and turn brushes that flick up the dirt into the container inside the cleaner. Very useful when you have power cuts and crumbs and dirt on the carpets!

When visiting the sales director one day he asked me to look at the latest improvement in the carpet sweeper handle. He gave me the new handle and said, 'Look at the screw.' The end of the handle that screwed into the cleaner body had an aluminium thread on it. This company had always fixed aluminium threads on the handles in preference to a screw turned in the actual wood of the handle. 'Yes,' I said, 'it's got an aluminium screw.'

'You don't understand do you!' he remonstrated. 'It's been moulded on. Not fixed as before – moulded. Moulded on to the end. It'll never come off. I've just got it from the factory about half an hour ago.'

'I can't see any difference,' I confessed.

'It's moulded,' he shouted, 'moulded on to the wood. We used to fix them with small screws. That moulded screw-end will always be part of the handle. The aluminium is now part of the wood.'

'I can just see the advertising,' I said. '"Our handles have moulded screw-ends. They'll never come off!" But the handles never came off before. What's new about this? I'm sorry, Bill, I think it's fine. It's a great achievement in the factory but it's simply a product attribute. You haven't any additional benefit for users because they didn't have any problems with loose handles before.'

I went on to recount that my grandmother had a competitive carpet sweeper made by Ewbank. Very, very old. Yet, although it had an ordinary turned thread in the wood to screw into the body of the cleaner, it had never given any trouble in about 30 years!

Like the bearer of bad news to potentates of old, I was not very popular that day. Nevertheless, to avoid facing the truth then would only have stored up problems for later on.

But, back to the first technique. It is used when you hear a point, requirement, need, objection, or whatever, mentioned by the prospect that exactly matches, or can be overcome, by a product benefit:

Customer: It's essential that we have a digital readout on the equipment.

The salesman knows that his latest model has a digital readout but what he does not say is, 'Ours has one!' He uses the first technique of repeating the point made, if necessary in slightly different form, and then linking it with the benefit:

Salesman: You're saying that you can only instal equipment with a digital readout?

Customer: Yes.

Salesman: I agree. [repeating the point] It's essential if you're going to have instant control over quality. That's why we have one on our new model 20. It also has a permanent recording device.

The essential step in the technique is, *repeat the point made* by the prospect and then link it with the product benefit.

Salesman: Good morning, Mr Prospect. I sent you a letter the other day to say I'd be giving you a ring this morning. I specialize in supplying a combined insurance and investment policy to business and professional people. This creates for you an immediate estate that never loses its value; after the second year it's a valuable savings account that always has cash available should you need it; should you fall ill and be unable to pay your premiums, it pays all future deposits; and you can retire any time after 55 with a guaranteed income.

Customer: I can make more money by investing it myself than you can make for me. I have £25,000 invested now that is yielding me a net thousand a year.

Salesman: [knows of a product benefit that can be linked with this prospect's desire to make his money work for him] That £25,000 nest-egg is important, Mr Prospect?

Customer: Certainly.

Salesman: You wouldn't object to doubling its value straight away?

Customer: Doubling it? To £50,000? What's the catch?

Salesman: No catch, Mr Prospect. I agree, you have a fine investment of £25,000 giving you a net thousand a year. You mustn't change that. But invest the £1,000 earnings a year into a £25,000 insurance investment plan and, immediately your estate is worth £50,000. What is more you have a savings account after two years and, should you fall ill or even if you are totally disabled, your future deposits are guaranteed. Normally you can retire any time after you're 55 with a very comfortable inflation-proof income.

It is clear that you must know all your product benefits and preferably have them on paper so that you can see them as you are talking on the phone.

You are selling mini-computer systems, we'll assume. One of the latest product attributes is a foolproof device that restricts entry into the system to the user or someone authorized by the user. The benefit is 100 per cent confidentiality of the contents of the system, restricted to those with authorization to access the material.

Your prospect tells you over the phone that his company must have complete confidentiality over its computer files and therefore they are thinking of buying a mainframe rather than several minis.

What you do not say at that point is that your company has this device that prevents unauthorized access into the system:

Salesman: I agree. Confidentiality is paramount in your business. Unauthorized access to your files would be disastrous. What you would really like to have is the flexibility of a number of minis but with the restricted access of a mainframe.

Customer: Exactly.

Salesman: Mr Prospect, that is why we have developed such a mini. Confidentiality is absolutely guaranteed – 100 per cent. No one you do not wish to can gain access to the files. You have the flexibility you need and the restricted access not previously available on such equipment.

You can almost feel yourself being drawn towards the product when the sales person restates the point you have made and then links it with the very product benefit you need!

Barrier building

The second technique is a more general one that you include during the whole of your sales presentation. It is 'barrier building'; a special form of barrier, not like the barriers to buying we have already discussed. You build barriers behind the prospect's statements so that he cannot retreat behind them. If, during the conversation he says that the colour must be blue, then later on you can use this and say, 'As you said sir, it has to be blue.' It is a barrier behind which he cannot retreat without contradicting himself:

Customer: The XYZ company are probably the most efficient in the industry.

Salesman: I agree, Mr Prospect. A very well-run company. They don't compete with you do they?

Customer: No. We just know them. The system we instal must be able to cope with almost as many variations as they have.

Salesman: Did you know that we have put in some of our equipment in part of their factory?

Customer: No, I didn't know that.

Salesman: Yes, they have our Rollastack and Stockmovers. And, as you said, they are probably the most efficient in the industry.

The barrier has been built. The prospect cannot now retreat and say that they are not efficient and is so helped to resolve his intention to satisfy the needs of his company. He is also moving towards a closing situation.

In the description of the first technique you can see how a barrier was built by the salesman saying, in effect, 'As you said, Mr Prospect, it is essential that the equipment has a digital readout.'

Barrier building is a technique that is used as you *listen*. You cannot use it without listening to what the prospect is saying. You are using the prospect's own utterances to build the barrier. It is a powerful method of helping the prospect to resolve to satisfy his or his company's needs by considering your product. And, if you develop this pleasantly and professionally, he will be much more inclined to place the business with you.

Self-examination questions on Chapter 7

7/1   Why is it necessary for the prospect to resolve to satisfy the need you have aroused?

7/2   What is the essential thing you have to do when telephoning a prospect, in order to be able to build barriers?

7/3   Before being able to link statements, objections and other points raised by the prospect with aspects of your product, what must you prepare?

7/4   When do you try to get the prospective buyer to resolve to satisfy the need you have established?

Chapter 8

How to Make the Offer

Making the offer means trying to close and get an order, an appointment, a definite enquiry, agreement to arrange a visit, permission to conduct a survey, to submit a quotation, or anything else that is relevant to your business. Never make an offer until the other person is ready to accept it or is prepared to consider it.

We have seen that there are two preliminary stages to cover before you make the offer: identifying the need and making sure that the prospect understands it, and resolution by the prospect to satisfy that need (see p 46). These may be explicit or implied. That is, you may actually state the need and the customer may say the words that mean he or she is resolving to satisfy the need that has been uncovered. Or, the need and its resolution may be implied in the language used.

The need and its resolution

Salesman: Good morning, sir. This is Smith of Fleet Cars. I understand you are interested in the new Super automatic.

Customer: Yes. Well, I called in at your High Street branch last Saturday, but they were a bit busy.

Salesman: Well, may I suggest you try it out, sir? We have a demonstration model here. I could bring it round to you whenever convenient ...

No! The offer has been made too early, and this creates an impression of pressure selling:

Salesman: Good morning, sir. This is Smith of Fleet Cars. I understand from one of my colleagues in our High Street branch that you might be interested in the new Super automatic.

Customer: Yes. I did call in there last Saturday but they were very busy.

Salesman: Have you a brochure on it, sir?

Customer: Yes. I picked it up on Saturday.

Salesman: Did you get a chance to look at the car, sir?

Customer: Not really. There were so many people there.

Salesman:	Can you spare some time during the week?
Customer:	Well, a little.
Salesman:	May I suggest, sir, I bring the car to you, then you can have a good look at it and try it out. Would a morning or afternoon be more convenient for you?

The salesman is certainly not going to sell the car on the phone in the sense that the customer gives him an order there and then. He has established that the customer is interested, that he has made the first approach, that he has not been able to inspect it properly and had resolved to do this when calling at the other branch.

The offer that the salesman makes is to bring the car to the customer for an inspection and test drive and he has only done this after a few preliminaries. He has judged, by the prospective customer's voice and answers on the phone, that the customer is 'in the market for a new car'; is resolved to have a look round to see what is available; is interested in a specific model.

The salesman might ask a further question before making the offer to take the car to the customer:

Salesman:	Do you have a little spare time this week, sir?
Customer:	Well, Tuesday or Wednesday. Today if you wish.

This indicates that the prospective customer is interested in looking further to resolve his need. The salesman would not then need to use the 'alternative close' – morning or afternoon? – because the customer has decided. He then puts the onus on the customer by getting him to make the decision:

Customer:	Could we make it about 11.00 tomorrow morning?
Salesman:	Of course, sir. Now, what address? [receives this and other details] What car do you run now, sir? [obtains this information] Nice car. How many miles has it done? [given] We could make you an attractive offer on that if you're interested, sir. Well then, until tomorrow at 11.00, sir. Thank you.

Here, the salesman is reinforcing the resolution made by the customer. He has hinted that the customer will obtain a satisfactory trade-in price for his present car. This increases the desire to purchase the new one.

As always, listen carefully to the answers made by the customer. He may only be interested if he can arrange a part-exchange with his present car; he may only be interested if he can get a good discount, and so on.

The responses and points made by the customer condition your replies. Before you make an offer ensure that the need has been established. If you don't, you are wasting your time and resources.

When selling on the phone it is very easy to imply that you are pressurizing the customer. To avoid this make sure she or he knows what the offer is and that there is no obligation. In other words, linked with your offer is absolute satisfaction guaranteed.

It is not like a face-to-face situation where an offer can be made and an official order given, or even cash handed over for the goods. On the phone, the prospect could agree to have the goods and then refuse to accept delivery or refuse to pay for them!

Making an offer on the telephone

This is a specialized area, largely built on confidence. Consider the following, in which a telesales woman is phoning a motor car distributor with the objective of getting him to advertise in the newspaper she represents. This telesales conversation actually happened, although the names have been changed to preserve the anonymity of the people and the newspaper concerned.

Note particularly how the woman opens the sale, how she tries to identify the customer's needs and how she identifies a completely different need from the one she was pursuing. She obtains resolution of the newly found need and finally makes the offer which the customer finds difficult to refuse!

Saleswoman: Good morning, Mr Peters, I'm Joan Black of the *News* advertising department. I see that you have been advertising recently in the ...

Customer: Yes, I have.

Saleswoman: May I ask, Mr Peters, whether you are having any success with your campaign?

Customer: Yes, quite good.

Saleswoman: I see one car you advertised was a very recent model with very low mileage. What colour is it?

Customer: Silver – metallic silver.

Saleswoman: And it's front wheel drive, isn't it? Does it have power steering?

Customer: Yes, also a first-class stereo radio. It's in absolutely showroom condition and under warranty.

Saleswoman: What about mileage?

Customer: Very low.

Saleswoman:	Those points don't come out in the ad, Mr Peters. Don't you think that …
Customer:	I don't know whether you're thinking of buying it, but you're too late. My son has decided to take it over!
Saleswoman:	Ah! I was going to suggest a slightly different approach, Mr Peters. Still, never mind. May I phone you in a week or so when we shall be planning a special feature which might interest you? Perhaps I could phone your secretary and arrange to call.
Customer:	I wish you could. I've just lost my secretary. She's been with me for the last 10 years. Her husband has landed a very good job in the Middle East.
Saleswoman:	[quick to realize a different and very urgent, real need] When will you be getting another one, Mr Peters?
Customer:	Early days yet. She only told me yesterday.
Saleswoman:	Have you thought of advertising in our special section dealing with top-class secretaries?
Customer:	No. But I guess that would be rather expensive.
Saleswoman:	But you would want a really first-class girl wouldn't you, sir?
Customer:	Of course. Tell me, what would a classified ad cost in that feature?
Saleswoman:	I can give the cost of that, Mr Peters, but I don't think that's the best way to get the kind of secretary you want. You should consider a semi-display ad. That's eight pounds a single column centimetre.
Customer:	So if I had something about two inches by two inches, what would that cost?
Saleswoman:	Mr Peters, you want a first-class secretary and you're in competition with every other successful business in the area. To attract the sort of girl you want you must take, I would suggest, a six-centimetre by two columns. That's twelve single-column centimetres – £96.
Customer:	Hm! Would that give me a large space compared with other ads?
Saleswoman:	Yes. You wouldn't be the largest but your advertisement would certainly catch the eye. But one insertion is certainly insufficient. I suggest that you take a series of four. …
Customer:	Wait a minute, I haven't even decided to put one in yet. You're talking about £400-worth of advertising.
Saleswoman:	Sorry, Mr Peters. I didn't finish. You are advertising for a top-flight secretary aren't you?

Customer: Yes.

Saleswoman: And you want to get hold of the best that's available?

Customer: Of course.

Saleswoman: And you'll want to see a number of applicants before you decide who is the best?

Customer: Yes.

Saleswoman: And you need to fill the post quickly.

Customer: That's for sure.

Saleswoman: That's the very reason I suggested a series of four. You will be certain of getting a sufficient number of replies from which to make a short list. And, if you fail to get satisfaction after the four insertions, we insert a fifth one free of charge. Furthermore, once you are satisfied, you can cancel any remaining insertions and you only pay for the ones you've had.

Customer: You mean that if I'm not satisfied after four insertions I get a £96 ad free?

Saleswoman: Yes. Or if you take a larger space – which I am not suggesting – you get the same size repeated. I must say though that, such is the pulling power of this particular section, it is unlikely that you will need four insertions. You will obtain a good number of really first-class applicants.

Customer: And if I order four and get someone after, say, two insertions, I can cancel the others and it will only cost me the two insertions?

Saleswoman: Exactly!

Customer: But I don't have anything prepared to put in the ad. I'm so busy. I don't have the time to do it. I think a small ad, a couple of lines will do.

Saleswoman: If the copy were all prepared for you and all you had to do were to let me know the salary range etc, that would get over that difficulty, wouldn't it? [a barrier has been built!]

Customer: Of course. But, as I said, I've no one here to do it.

Saleswoman: Mr Peters, I'm used to preparing copy and also sketching layouts. I can knock this into shape for you very quickly. In fact, I can call to see you either this afternoon or tomorrow morning. Which would be the more convenient?

First the offer of the insertion in the special feature they are having, then the offer to prepare the copy for the ad, then the offer to call and clinch the deal. Skilled and yet easy when you know how to progress the sale.

Only make the offer when you have identified the need and the customer realizes what he or she needs.

Self-examination questions on Chapter 8

8/1   You should never make an offer to a prospective customer until ... until when?

8/2   If you lose orders it will be because you are failing to close strongly. Do you agree?

8/3   What do you think is meant by 'talking yourself out of the order'?

Chapter 9

Assessment of the Offer – Dealing With Objections

You are on the phone to your prospect, you have said good-day to him, you have opened the sales presentation, discovered his need, obtained his understanding and he is resolved to satisfy that need, you have made the offer – then come the objections!

It is the buyer's job to buy as keenly as possible and to buy the best quality product in line with the company's policy. In fact, the buyer is not doing his job unless he uses his best endeavours to buy at the keenest possible price. Raising objections is second nature to him.

For example, you will never hear a buyer say to you: 'I like your product very much, but your price is too low. If you can put it up by about 15 per cent, I'll place the business with you'!

Always your price is too high. Always they want a discount. Even when you have got beyond that stage, and the order is about to be placed, the purchasing director enters the scene and he wants to justify his position by demonstrating that he has got an extra $2\frac{1}{2}$ per cent from the supplier!

Don't become worried if objections arise when you are phoning prospects. On the other hand, don't take the view that used to be taught, that you should welcome them because they prove that the prospect is interested in your product. It's not necessarily true! However, if the prospect is stating one or two objections, at least he is still on the phone with you.

Helping the buyer

Many objections arise during the assessment stage. It is your job as a salesperson to help the buyer to make a decision. If you are trying to get an appointment, help the prospect to agree to seeing you. Make it easy for him to fit you in. Don't do what one salesman did:

Salesman: Mr Prospect, I can call at any time to suit you. When may I come along?

Customer: This Thursday at 8.30 would be fine.

Salesman: Ah! That's a little awkward for me.... [pause] I'm afraid I can't manage that.

Then why should he say he could call at any time to suit? To suit himself obviously. If he means it, he must stick to it. If you say that you can call any time but that there are exceptions, say so: 'I can call at any time to suit you, except this Thursday morning until after 11.00.'

When this salesman was telling this story his attitude was, 'Of all the times I could have seen him, he chose the one day when I have to take the kids to school.'

It's also an example of one of the many facets of 'Murphy's Law'. You will meet it frequently. If there's only one time when it's really inconvenient for you, that's the time the other person will choose!

When you have made an offer to the prospect in your telesales presentation that, as far as you can ascertain, fits in with the prospect's needs, you will have reached the stage of assessment. It is usually at this point that the prospect starts to raise objections.

Valid objections

While invalid objections can usually be answered fairly easily, valid ones cannot readily be dealt with by simple answers. Unanswerable objections usually take one of two forms: 'I have no money', or, 'I have no need.'

The secret of dealing with objections is *treat every objection as valid* and deal with it accordingly.

Do not assume that the objection raised is a stall – there is no way you can know this. If you react as though you think it is a stall, you can very easily antagonize the prospect. Whereas, if you treat the objection as valid and respond professionally to it, the prospect cannot take offence. In fact, you can frequently manoeuvre this to your advantage. If you treat an objection on its merits and the prospect really was raising it as a stall, he will often feel the need to compensate later in the discussions. Let us examine some of the more usual objections and suggestions for dealing with them.

Objection: No need because too much stock

The only way you can help the prospect to overcome this objection is to close for an appointment and then see how you can help *him* to sell stock. By that means *you*, in turn, will be able to sell to him:

Prospect: Sorry, but until we can shift some of our present stocks, we're not buying any more.

You: Mr Prospect, you will know far better than I that products held in stock cost money – they don't earn money. I have one or two ideas that might help you to shift them. Would it be all right if I call round this afternoon to see you in person ... or would you prefer a morning?

Objection: We have no call for your product

This is a common objection especially if you are selling to dealers. There are a number of ways you can deal with this:

You: Tell me, Mr Prospect, do you ever have any call for haircuts? I doubt it. But, if you put a large, illuminated hairdressing sign outside your store, you would! If you display our pack, it's so well known, you'd get a call for it.

You: If we only stocked those goods we get a call for, Mr Prospect, our business would stand still. If you get a call for a product before you stock it, would your customer wait until you could supply it? I doubt it. The customer would buy from your competitor and that would open up the opportunity for buying other things from your competitor. Before you know it, you've lost a customer.

Objection: No room for a new line

This is said by most dealers who have all their available space being used. If you think about it, the stocking of goods is a problem of selection. The dealer must stock those goods that are going to sell. If he stops buying when his available space is filled up, how does he know that he has the variety of goods that will sell? Some of his lines may stay occupying space that could otherwise be utilized by your product:

You: Of course you don't have any room, Mr Prospect. You wouldn't be as good a businessman as you are if you did have room. No one should stock a new line until they know what it will make per square metre for them. When I show you what returns can be made on this new product – all backed by the experience of others – I think you'll find that you'll want to stock it. I can assure you, it doesn't stay in stock long.

Objection: We're satisfied with our present supplier thank you. There's no reason to change

A difficult one. Develop well-burnished responses to this objection. The main thrust of your answers must be to persuade the buyer that it is good policy to have alternative sources of supply just in case something happens with his present source. You must ascertain who is the present supplier:

You: May I ask who supplies you now, Mr Prospect?

Prospect: [names supplier]

You: They are a good company, sir. Many of my customers also
            buy from them. Just recently, I was talking with one of our
            good customers who splits his orders between them and us.
            Whenever one of us has problems with deliveries, which can
            happen to all of us, as you know, he is never short of stock
            because of his second sourcing policy. I think you'll agree
            that's sound. Now, so that you'll be aware of our current
            range, may I put our latest catalogue in the post? We could
            then see which products you could have as a back-up?

Objections to the product are frequent:

**Objection: We know of another company that brought your product but
they were not happy with it**
You cannot deny this. You don't know. You must find out the facts.
Get the complaint out into the open. Ask what, specifically, was the
problem:

You: This is the first I have heard of this, Mr Prospect, and I'll take
            it up with my company and the customer right away. May I
            ask who it was please?

Objections are sometimes similar to complaints. Don't deny them,
don't contradict them, don't ridicule them. Listen to them, establish
the facts, stay cheerful, be glad that you can put things right, say you
will deal with it right away. Sometimes product objections are
broad-based attitudes tinged with prejudice. You cannot deal with
this over the phone. You must go for an appointment close. You
must try to get a personal interview with this objector. The best
strategy is to get the prospect to agree to a trial usage.

Prospect: We've used a Simpson for a long time and prefer it.

You: A first-class machine, Mr Prospect. It gives good results. I would
            like to know more about it in comparison with ours. You're a fair-
            minded person, Mr Prospect, I'd appreciate it if you would give our
            machine a fair trial and let me know how it compares with the other.
            May I call and discuss it?

With some products, of course, you cannot arrange for a trial. And,
if the prospect has been using the same product for a long time,
changing attitudes can be difficult. Your best course of action here
is to search for those reasons why the prospect maintains loyalty to
the competitive product:

You: Yes, a first-class product, Mr Prospect. Some of my custo-
            mers think similarly about mine, others think so about the

one you use. Tell me, sir, what is it you particularly like about that product?

By getting the prospect to outline the features about the competition, you can modify your subsequent telesales presentations knowing what to stress in your product! You will also learn whether such loyalty to the competitive product is based on sound reasons or is a manifestation of prejudice or habit.

Classification of objections

- Imagined objections
- Pretend objections – excuses
- Real, sincere objections.

Your first task is to find out the real nature of the objection. To do this adequately you must consider it in relation to the objective you have set yourself.

Let us review some of the things we are trying to achieve when we make a phone call:

- To obtain information
- To make an appointment to call on the prospect
- To sell something, which really means getting authorization to deliver something to the prospect in the expectation that it will be paid for
- To obtain agreement to submit a quotation
- To have our company's name put on their potential suppliers' list
- To progress the sale.

Never be too rigid about your objective. You might start out with one objective and find, during the conversation, that it is appropriate to change it. A simple example will illustrate:

Salesman: Good afternoon, Mr Prospect. Philpot of Acme Manufacturing. I am in your area next week and wonder if you are free to see me?

Customer: Ah! Good afternoon, Mr Philpot. Glad you phoned. We are getting short of single round-ended blue slabs. How soon could you deliver, say, a complete load?

Obviously, Philpot is going to change his objective. And, remember how the saleswoman on the newspaper quickly spotted a new need for the car distributor and sold him on a series of ads for a new secretary (see Chapter 8).

Imagined objections

Prospects often advance objections that have no real substance. These are imaginary and usually the result of faulty communications. You should be able to detect this if the objection raised does not follow from what you have said, is not valid or is the result of someone feeding the prospect with untrue information:

Salesman: [his objective is to explain his company's total system and obtain a date to put on a demonstration in the prospect's factory] That's how we can revolutionize your whole design and manufacturing system, Mr Prospect.

Customer: I'm sorry there's no way we could undertake such a major investment at this time. I don't think there's any advantage in your putting on a demonstration.

Salesman: [deciding it's an imaginary objection] Mr Prospect, what do you understand to be the minimum investment necessary to start this system?

Customer: From what you have been saying ... [pause] ... I suppose we're in the half-million bracket.

So it is an untrue objection. Possibly it might have been fed to the prospect by a competitor who is trying to sell on price. But you don't simply scoff and say that your equipment doesn't cost anything like that amount. You allow the prospect to 'save face':

Salesman: Mr Prospect, you'd be most unwise to consider a total investment of that magnitude. It must be done in a controlled manner over a period of time, as the design and product people learn to handle the new technology. Design first, then draughting and then implementation in the production process. The whole system would take at least three years to complete. The design stage, which is what I am suggesting you consider, need not involve you in more than about £25,000 and that would be over a year. Then the cost of the total system would depend on how far it's possible to take in your production. However, once you have the design system installed and working, your design time is cut dramatically, with a great saving in design costs, certainly at least the £25,000.

Customer: Hm!

Salesman: Tell me, is £25,000 stretching your budget too far?

Customer: Not really.

65

Salesman: Because if it is, you could lease the equipment and upgrade it as necessary. May I suggest that you have a look at the demonstration first? Obviously you're not committing yourself in any way, and then you can decide where we go from there. What about, say, three weeks on Tuesday? The 1st.

And so the imaginary objection was dealt with. Another:

Customer: No I prefer not to install your machine. It doesn't run as fast as the XYZ machine.

Salesman: That's perfectly true, Mr Prospect. Our machine only has to be serviced every six months. We have compromised slightly on speed in order to increase the overall usage time. As you know, downtime with these machines is a very costly business so we designed it with the total operating cost in mind. If you ran the two machines side by side for a year do you have any idea of the saving that our machine would show you over any other machine on the market?

I am not going to give you a series of success stories and demonstrate that you can overcome every imaginary objection. Imagination is a very powerful human ability. You have to remain flexible and responsive to every objection made by the prospect.

If you judge that it is an imaginary objection, then it is likely that the prospect does not have sufficient data from you or does not fully understand the proposition you have been explaining.

Your line of response must be based on open probes followed by closed questions so that you can narrow down the objection made to its real root.

Pretend objections or excuses

These are not real objections but part of the defensive mechanism of the prospect. The best way to deal with pretend objections is to assume that they are real and treat them as such with the buyer. This is known as 'calling his bluff'. To give an extreme example:

Customer: I'm sorry, I'm afraid I'm too busy to see you at the moment; we are absolutely up to our eyes in work. Please leave it for a month or so.

Salesman: I understand, Mr Prospect. You'd like me to leave it for a while?

Customer: If you wouldn't mind.

Salesman: Of course not. Do you have your diary handy?

Customer: Yes.

Salesman: [stating a month that is more than six or seven months away]

> What about a date in, say, next December. How are you
> fixed?

The customer is now not sure whether you are serious or not. There are so many ways in which this can develop. You have to remain cool and serious unless the prospect laughs. But you are calling his bluff.

This prospect also has an excuse that he is too busy to see you:

Customer: I'm sorry. It sounds good but I really don't have the time.

Salesman: I understand, Mr Prospect. Would it be any use joining me for lunch? Do you like a pie and coffee or something, or is there somewhere closer to your office where we could get something quickly? I don't need the whole lunch-time to tell you my story – just about five minutes, so I won't be boring you.

It is always advisable to offer 'coffee or something', implying that you are ready to buy him something stronger. If you offer a 'drink', you might easily offend the customer who may have strong views about drinking during the lunch-hour. Also, if you are visiting customers after lunch, rather than phoning, you should never drink alcohol during lunch-time.

You overcome pretend objections by listening and developing more information for the prospect to think about. There are a number of ways that this can develop. He might meet you for lunch. He might even say that he is too busy to eat! He might say he brings lunch and eats in. Suppose he said this and you have done your research thoroughly, even to knowing the local eating places near to his office:

Customer: Thanks very much, but I bring lunch and eat in.

Salesman: I see, Mr Prospect. Every day?

Customer: Yes.

Salesman: Do you like old fashioned steak and kidney pie with real home-made pastry?

Customer: [laughing] Yes!

Salesman: Well, why not have a change today? I know of a little place not far from your office where I often eat at midday. Their steak and kidney pie is really first class. It's home-made. But you have to get there early otherwise it's all gone. What about letting me pick you up about quarter to half twelve?

The salesman has changed his objective slightly. He is now trying to achieve the objective of getting the prospect to join him for lunch.

Customer: It's very nice of you but I don't really think that I can.

Salesman: All right, Mr Prospect. I realize you're busy. Maybe you can join me another time when the pressure eases a little. My proposition might just help you reduce that pressure. Tell me, when could you fit in just five minutes to see me? I'll put my watch on the table between us and prove it.

Don't give up. When you get excuses, probe and get to the real root of the objection. Where you think it appropriate, call the person's bluff and listen carefully to the responses. The excuse you will meet most of the time will be the 'too busy to see you' excuse. Only you, with your knowledge of your company and its products will be able to develop responses to this ploy.

Real objections

These must be dealt with as soon as possible. If you ignore one, it will remain a permanent obstacle to the transaction. If you don't dispose of real objections to the satisfaction of the prospect, they will stay at the back of the mind and often become the 'real', hidden reason for not closing the sale with you.

Sometimes the objection is real but of a nature whereby you can turn it to good use:

Salesman: [talking on the phone with the engineer in the factory] Mr Prospect, I'm with the RST Valve company. I asked if I could have a quick talk with you. We supply valves.

Customer: Ah! I don't buy valves.

Salesman: But, you use a number of valves in the organization, don't you?

Customer: Yes. But I don't buy the valves.

Salesman: But if you had to say which valves gave the company the most headaches would you say it would be the high pressure outlets?

Customer: Yes, that's true. But, as I said, I don't buy valves.

Salesman: Do you think that the buyer who buys them would be interested in a valve that would reduce your downtime due to valve failure?

Customer: Well, yes.

Salesman: Could you tell me who I should speak to, sir? And may I tell him that I have had a brief word with you on the subject?

The greater number of real objections, whether factual or part of the buying ploy by the prospect, will be objections to price. Now, you can always reduce your price. Buyers will be only too pleased. They are always after price reductions. Let's follow a typical sequence:

Salesman: [phoning a prospect to whom he has sent a quotation for the product] Hullo, Mr Prospect, I trust you received the quotation.

Customer: Yes, thank you. I like your product, but I'm afraid you're out on price.

What an unusual response! However, we assume that this is a real, sincere objection and the price is too high. The question we would really like to be answered is, 'How much are we out?' If we knew that we could then consider dropping the price if it's not too much, so as to get the business. But, this is the one question you must *not* ask unless you know the prospect very, very well.

You must judge the situation carefully because you might offend an old friend by putting the direct question: 'How much out are we, Tom?' Even an old friend will appreciate a professional approach.

Suggested general approach
Before using this ploy, you must know your product, its price structure, policy on discounts, the market, and competition, the importance of which have already been discussed in Chapter 7.

Salesman: What would you consider should be the price for this particular product?

There are only three possible answers he can give to this question: a price that is acceptable to you there and then; a price that is very low, almost ridiculously low; or a price that is reasonable, but lower than you can accept.

Customer: I wouldn't expect to pay more than £95 each for these.

Either you can accept the order at this price or you can't. Let us say for the moment that you can accept the order at £95. You do *not* jump in and say: 'I can let you have it at £95'. Instead repeat the statement:

Salesman: I see. You're saying that £95 is about the right price for this product?

Customer: Yes.

Salesman: [now, using the other technique, builds a barrier] If it were possible for me to offer them at £95, you could have placed the order? [note particularly the use of the word 'were', and the tense used in the second half of the sentence: 'could have placed the order']

69

Customer: Yes. [this is now a barrier behind which he cannot retreat and say that £95 is too high]

Salesman: [pauses] OK, sir. I'm prepared to put the order through at £95 but I'll need an order number now.

The second possible response to your original question is a price well below what you can accept and probably such a low price that he is 'trying it on'. In effect, he is saying that he can get it for less. You should know all the competitive products and their prices. And, we assume that the price you have quoted is keen, fair and very reasonable. If you are quoting high prices compared with comparable quality on the market, then this passage has no meaning for you.

Salesman: As low as that. Now that does interest me, sir. Would you mind telling me which model you can get at that price?

Either he does or he doesn't. If he doesn't, you must be able to reel off all the important, comparable products and their prices to prove that you really do know the market, you know all the products that compete with your company and you know their prices. And their prices are equal to, or higher than yours.

There is a real marketing point here. The product he mentions at the very low price may be of a quality that is satisfactory for his needs. If so, then your company must review its product policy. There is no sense in operating in a market with a product of too high a quality. On the other hand, the buyer may need to be educated in the use of the product. It could be that the product needs to possess a minimum number of attributes to work satisfactorily in all situations.

The prospect may be saying, in effect, 'It's not worth that much.' He is then not so much comparing with the competition, but possibly displaying his ignorance of the market. If the prospect says that it is not worth the price you are asking, this is because his concept of quality is lower than your price and lower than that generally prevailing on the market.

It isn't that your price is too high; his idea of quality is too low.

Justifying the price
You have to explain what it is you are selling. One of the most powerful methods of dealing with price objections of this type is to show that by the use of the product, the price is very quickly recovered by the savings made.

Another method is to break the price into smaller units. All products can be shown as a price per week, even a price per day or a price per customer product.

The third possible answer is that he mentions a price that could be considered as fair but is below what you can accept. You must then explore the initial price, the operating costs, maintenance costs, service costs, installation costs if appropriate, delivery, allowances and any trade-ins, terms of payment, credit given; the whole range of costs.

The concept you must transmit to the prospect is 'cost of ownership'. It isn't the initial outlay. It's also the cost of running and the cost of keeping it in first-class working condition.

The reply, 'We can't afford it' is perhaps the one genuine objection – assuming that it's true. This is an entirely different response and you must then assume that, if the prospect had the money, he would buy the product from you. You would have worked out beforehand some attractive financial packages whereby the product could be acquired at your price.

Quality is remembered long after the price has retreated into the background. If price is still remembered, it becomes part of the pride of possession. People often ask, 'What do you think of this?' and, after the murmurs of approval and approbation, 'You know, that cost me ...!'

Always have adequate financial suggestions or packages you can propose to the prospect if you meet a genuine objection to initial price:

Salesman: As I understand it, Mr Prospect, you would like to have our product but the price is over your budget.

Customer: Yes, I'm afraid it is. [barrier built]

Salesman: We can arrange for you to lease this through our own finance company if it would help. Of course, you would have the advantage of including such costs in your annual operating costs.

Whenever you meet an objection to price and the prospect says that he likes your product, but that you are out on price, the one question you really need answered is, 'What do you really mean?'

If, after all your endeavours, the prospect still says, 'Fine, but can I have a discount', there are only three possible answers: 'No', 'Yes', and 'I don't know'.

With 'No', you risk everything. You have to restate in summary form why he should place the business with you. You should ask how could the product be modified or what things could be removed from it to reduce its price. As it stands, there is no discount.

'Yes', means that you must have pre-calculated and know what it is you can offer. Don't give this too early in the negotiations or you will be asked for more!

'I don't know', is your last chance to retrieve the situation. As far as you are concerned you tell the prospect that you are unable to offer a discount. If you are negotiating a worthwhile order and there is still the objection to price and a discount is demanded, you can suggest a meeting is arranged with one of your more senior executives.

All these comments assume that your price is a fair one for the product. Above all, be convincing on the phone when you mention price. Don't be afraid of your price and do not use vague words such as 'more or less', 'roughly', 'approximately', 'almost', 'sort of'. Be concrete. Nearly a hundred years ago John Ruskin wrote: 'There is hardly anything in the world that some man cannot make a little worse and sell a little cheaper; and the people who consider price only, are this man's lawful prey.'

Self-examination questions on Chapter 9

9/1 Do you think that you should help the prospect to assess the proposition you have put to him?

9/2 What three possible ways might the prospect answer your question, 'What would you consider to be an acceptable price?'

9/3 During the sales presentation when are objections most likely to arise?

9/4 What is the best way to deal with objections?

Chapter 10

How to Get the Decision

Getting the decision does not necessarily mean getting the order. It means getting the respondent to decide on the objective you set yourself before you picked up the phone.

Obviously you will know whether it is normal practice to obtain an order on the phone in your type of business and, if so, you may have this as an objective. Getting the decision in this case would be getting the order. If you have something special to offer the customer your objective might be to obtain a larger order than usual.

When you close a sale you are achieving what you set out to do. It may mean getting the order but, if you consider the thousands of types of transactions that take place every hour of the day throughout the world, you will realize that only a very small fraction will result in orders on the first call.

More face-to-face sales presentations than telephone calls end in orders, simply because the product and its uses can be demonstrated. There can be various kinds of decision you want from respondents on the phone. You may want to obtain an order for a relatively small quantity; to set up a special window display in the prospect's business; to get support for a cooperative advertising venture; to arrange for a further delivery of the product you are already supplying; to get agreement to submit a quotation; to make an appointment for a representative to call.

Create the right state of mind

If your prospect is at all agitated, it is unlikely that you will reach agreement because the prospect will be in a negative mood, ready to disagree with everything and everyone. This antipathy will create a natural obstacle to agreement with you. Put the prospect at ease so that he or she does not feel that something is being suggested that is against his or her will:

Salesman: I trust you had a good break.
Prospect: Oh! Excellent.

Salesman:	Did you have any rain during the two weeks?
Prospect:	Just a light shower one day. Apart from that it was hot every day.
Salesman:	And the food and everything was fine?

By this simple and genuine enquiry about the prospect's holiday you can create a relaxed atmosphere. If you were told where the prospect was going on holiday, you should have kept a note of it. By linking your enquiry with your knowledge: 'I trust you had a good break in Greece', you will be demonstrating a real interest in the other person and this, coupled with other professional skills, puts you well above your competitors. However, consider the following conversation:

Salesman:	I trust you had a good break.
Prospect:	Disaster!
Salesman:	What happened? [sits back knowing that the prospect is going to use a lot of the phone call to let off steam]
Prospect:	[relates all that happened on the vacation, salesman listens carefully as though it is a complaint]
Salesman:	So you don't feel as though you've had a holiday. You need another one to get over it!

Although this is not a complaint against your company, you must treat it in the same way. You must hear out the complaint but avoid becoming involved by agreeing with the prospect. Remember, that your prospect selected it! Be sympathetic and understanding. Simply ask for explanations and enquire how the prospect reacted to the situations he describes. If you become involved in the conversation and a party to the condemnation of the resort, you are not an objective observer. You will not be able to put the prospect at ease, you will inflame the disaster:

Salesman:	I trust you had a good break.
Prospect:	Disaster!
Salesman:	Oh yes! You went to Malidorm, didn't you? I've never heard a good report about that place. A pal of mine was there earlier in the year and ...

How not to win friends and influence people! You can almost see the prospect bristling and ready to let rip on his condemnation of the resort in general and the hotel in particular. And he is certainly not going to be in a relaxed mood which must be your first aim if you are to get a favourable decision.

Hearing the facts

Make sure that the prospect has the chance to hear all the facts. But don't assume that the prospect has to have them all to make a decision. Perhaps more importantly, don't assume that the decision will be made on what *you* consider are the main points. There may be a small point which has special appeal to the prospect and on which the close can be made. Listen carefully for appropriate responses when you are describing the proposition and, as soon as you detect a side issue in which the prospect is interested, try to close on that:

Salesman: Well, I'm glad you had a good time. Perhaps you can let me have the address of the hotel sometime. Good. Now, you'll probably have seen our quotation. Does the specification match what you are looking for?

Prospect: Yes. Although your price is a little high.

Salesman: [ignoring the objection] There are only two others on the market that can match your needs exactly: especially the restriction of entry by unauthorized personnel.

Prospect: Well, that's vital as far as we are concerned.

Salesman: It's probably also why our second-hand machines keep their prices so well.

Prospect: I didn't know you did second-hand machines.

Salesman: Oh yes. A lot of our customers like to upgrade their machines as their business grows. Y'know, come to think of it, we don't sell new machines! All our machines have been thoroughly used. We don't sell one until it's been in use on our test bench for at least a month. But all the quality control in the world won't really substitute for the machine actually being in use. And, as they're built to a high spec, you're buying proven quality. That's why the machines we take back in part-exchange keep their value.

The prospect is now interested in side-issues and the salesman is able to close by asking when the machine can be delivered for test on the prospect's premises. Always listen to responses. They will often indicate the points on which you can close and get the decision you want.

Understanding the proposition

If you are seeking an appointment and then a demonstration at his

75

factory, pause at each stage and check that the two stages and what will be involved on his side are understood:

Salesman: As I said, Mr Prospect, I could call and make a quick survey with you and the design engineer. This would take about an hour to an hour and a half. Then I could arrange a convenient time for the demonstration. [checking] For my survey, can we agree on a day, say, next week?

Customer: Yes, Thursday would be a good day. John will be available then, too.

Salesman: Fine. For the demonstration, your drawing office and works people should be present. We would need about a week to organize this at our end. Would, say, the 25th or 26th be of any use to you?

And so on through the conversation because, although it sounds as though this salesman has achieved his objective, the prospect has not yet said a definite 'yes'. He can still change his mind and say that it all seems a little involved and difficult, what with the holidays, people away on visits and courses, and not least that he has to get off his chair and organize something outside of his normal work! Make sure that the prospect understands the proposition, what he will have to do, when, what it will cost, if anything, and when it will happen.

What will happen

Tell the prospect what is going to happen. Instruct him. Make it easy for him to sit back and simply say, 'yes'. If it's all new to him, treat him as you would treat a student being shown how to manipulate algebraic formulae for the first time:

Salesman: Fine, madam. Now I'll arrange for Mr Grant to call on Tuesday. He'll be able to measure up and tell you exactly how much you'll need. Then, you can look at the patterns he'll bring with him. They're all marked with their grades and prices so you will know how much it will cost. He will be with you about 10.30. Is that all right?

Salesman: Right then, Mr Kempton. I'll put the syllabus in the post to you tomorrow; you'll reserve the hotel room for Wednesday the 28th and arrange for coffee, lunch and afternoon tea. We shall also need an overhead projector, an acetate roll or separate sheets, a screen and a spare lamp. I'll be there early and organize the layout of the room. I'll bring all the handouts, the aids and everything. All you need to do is to get your people there ready to start promptly at 9.00. OK?

Varying use of words

If you have to repeat some or all of your sales presentation, use different words to stress the main points of your proposition. If you see a film for the second or third time, you always notice something you had not seen before. It is the same with a sales presentation. The first time the prospect hears only one or two points, the second time he hears other advantages. As you repeat the points, the whole message begins to take shape in his mind.

Don't be afraid of having a little silence here and there. If you make a telling point, let it sink in by saying nothing. Unbroken silence can do a lot in helping to close a sale because it allows the prospect to think about what you have just said. This means that you must know when you have to carry out one of the most difficult tasks of a salesperson – to stop talking!

You have doubtless heard politicians who, on being asked a question, make a statement that relates to the question but is what they would really like to have been asked; construct a reply to the questions raised by the statement; reinforce it with evidence that is frequently far removed from the original topic but appears to add credence to what has been said thus far; justify the way in which they have made their reply and add a few paragraphs of comment which sometimes mean they end up talking about something which has nothing whatsoever to do with the original question!

They are the chief exponents of the long, rambling response. It seems to be the norm for politics. It will not do in selling, especially on the phone. Short, succinct responses to the point. Then stop! Here are the earlier instructions repeated, stressing the main points:

Salesman: So, madam, Mr Grant will have a full range of samples from which you can choose. They are all priced, so after he has measured up, you can see how much it will cost to do it in any of the samples. He'll see you at 10.30 Tuesday morning.

Salesman: OK, Mr Kempton. You'll have the syllabus the day after tomorrow, by which time you'll have booked the room for Wednesday the 28th. And you'll arrange for the overhead projector. If you can't get the acetate roll, a pack of fifty sheets will do. You'll make sure there's a spare lamp for the projector. [pause and listen and, depending on what Kempton says, repeat the remainder] Don't worry about the room layout; I'll see to that. I'll bring the handouts and other aids with me. You'll have your people there for me to start at 9.00.

Maintaining a positive attitude

Always look on the bright side; even when things are not going too well, look for the few things that are positive. When talking with a prospect on the phone do not follow the prospect into the negative areas which he or she is raising. Listen carefully and see what positive points can be taken from the situation. Smile as you say things – this will certainly help.

Closing signals

These come in all shapes and sizes. It depends on the product, the offer you have made, the personality of the prospect, the way you have presented your case:

'You'd be prepared to do this next week?'

'Would you need our works engineer present?'

'Delivery would be guaranteed in three days?'

'And it would only take about an hour and a half?'

'I do have a little time on Tuesday morning.'

'I wouldn't be able to visit your office.'

How do you detect a closing signal? By *listening*!

Using the telephone to get decisions

The telephone is being used to get decisions by one company whose salesmen used to make an average of 35 calls a week and win an average of $3\frac{1}{2}$ new customers a month. Put another way, the salesmen used to make an average of about 42 appointments to get one new customer.

With the help of a team of telephonists the salesmen now need only 14 appointments to get a new customer and the average number of new customers obtained each month is six.

The salesmen's working schedule is controlled by telephonists who each have a computer terminal and call up prospects according to priorities laid down by the marketing team.

The telephonist gets the name of the person responsible for purchasing the type of equipment the company is selling and finds out what they already possess. This also provides a useful market survey. Approximately 25 per cent of the calls have to be re-made because the buyer was not available but 10 per cent of all calls result in appointments being made with decision makers in good prospective customers.

When the appointments are made, information on the prospect is printed out for the salesmen. Unproductive visits are recorded on the printouts and returned for re-entry into the computer file. Files are continually kept up to date; prospects going out of business or becoming customers are removed and new prospects added.

The cost is relatively low: the combined cost of the telephonists, the telephone bill and the use of a computer comes to approximately 15 per cent of the salesmen's salary.

Orders are not often achieved on the first appointment with customers but two-thirds of the abortive first calls have been eliminated. The telephone is being used to get more decisions from genuine prospects.

Getting a decision on the phone is the result of a carefully planned operation.

Self-examination questions on Chapter 10

10/1   When you speak on the phone with a customer you know well and he tells you of his poor holiday, should you sympathize with him?

10/2   What is one of the most difficult things for a salesman to do?

10/3   All the time you are speaking with people on the phone you are advised to do something continually. What is it?

10/4   What value is there in repeating the main points of your sales presentation?

Chapter 11

How to Communicate Effectively

Most activities would cease if there was no communication. The basic considerations are that communication is a means to an end, it is *not* an end in itself, and that there are degrees of importance of communication. Consider the difference between 'Fire!' and 'Take the cake out of the oven when it's cooked.' When someone shouts 'Fire', it is expected that action will be taken immediately. You do not enter into a discussion about it; you make for the nearest exit. Fire is not negotiable.

When you are talking on the phone with someone, you expect to get an immediate reaction to your requests and questions. This means that your presentation must be well prepared, simple to understand and easy to act on.

The risk of a communication breakdown when using the phone, is reduced because you are operating on a one-to-one basis and can keep a constant check to ensure that the respondent understands. You should check that the main points of your conversation are understood by using this five-point plan:

- What is suggested to be done
- When, where and, if necessary, how
- Who is going to do it
- At what cost
- Benefits – cash and non-cash.

These cover all the main issues of any proposal. If you are reporting to superiors in your organization on a proposed venture, using these five points will enable them to understand what you are suggesting very quickly.

If you have to prepare a written report, this same five-point plan will help you to cover the main things that have to be considered before a decision may be taken.

When using the telephone to sell, to make appointments, or to do anything, remember to check that your respondent knows what it is you are proposing; when and where this will happen and, if appropriate, how it will be done; whether you or someone else will do it; what it will cost; what benefits the respondent will get by agreeing.

Sample survey conversation

Here is a conversation between a consultant and his customer who has commissioned him to survey some of the customer's clients. The five-point plan – what, when, who, cost, benefits – is used as a basis for checking that all is agreed:

Customer: Do you think you could spend the two weeks in the area talking with the clients in one go, rather than take two separate weeks?

Consultant: Yes. I'd prefer that. I'll travel on the Sunday so that I can start first thing Monday. You'll have arranged all the interviews by then won't you?

Customer: Yes. That's no problem. We can fix about 12 for each week.

Consultant: Good. That's 24 for the two weeks. Will they all be in the same area?

Customer: No. Some will be in the north but the main ones will be near Glasgow or Edinburgh.

Consultant: Fine. To reduce travelling, I take it you'd book me into the most convenient hotels near to the clients?

Customer: Yes. I think we need to put you in at two; one just north of Glasgow and one north of Edinburgh: somewhere quiet, I expect you'd prefer.

Consultant: Thank you. Yes. Can we meet on the Sunday evening? Perhaps dinner?

Customer: Certainly.

Consultant: I'd like to have a full brief on the clients I'll be seeing for, say, Monday, Tuesday and Wednesday.

Customer: That's no problem.

Consultant: Good. We've agreed the fee. How would you like the hotel bills paid? Will you see to it, or shall I pay and let you have the bills?

Customer: Whichever you like.

Consultant: I'll pay, then, and let you have them at the end of each week. Then, any private phone calls I have or other personal items, I can settle separately. I'd like to have progress meetings with you on the Wednesday and Friday evenings to make sure that we're all talking the same language.

Customer: Sure. That's fine.

Consultant: At the end of the two weeks I'll prepare a report on each of your clients, and any others that I see during the period, and suggest the action we take.

Customer: Splendid.

Consultant: Now. I'll be driving up; arriving at the hotel about 6.00 on Sunday. That's the 14th. And see you for dinner. Say, about 7.30?

Customer: Yes. That's OK.

Notice how the five-point plan has been used to cover the main points and that the respondent – the customer – has agreed those points. There's one other thing you should always introduce – an 'insurance policy'. Consider:

Customer: Yes. That's OK.

Consultant: Just in case we need to contact each other before I see you on the Sunday, will you note this number, please – 0234, that's the STD for Borchester, 7722. OK? [listens to the repeating of the number] And where could I get hold of you if I'm delayed with a puncture or something? [listens, repeats the number as writing it down]

Sales sentences

Develop a number of sales sentences for each section of your presentation. To start with, you should develop a range of openings and have these prominently displayed in front of you, so that you can refer to them when phoning. You will find that you naturally develop just two or three. Here, I am developing an opening that I could use if I were to phone you and try to sell you a course on telephone selling:

'If you were able to develop more sales by using the phone in your present job, would this be of interest to you?'

'If you were able to get more sales by a more persuasive use of the phone, would this help you in your present job?'

'Do you find using the phone helps you in your job to get sales?'

'Would using the phone to get more business be a cost saving for you?'

'Is it possible to increase your sales by stronger selling on the telephone?'

'Would it be possible to increase your sales by greater use of the telephone?'

'How much do you use your phone now to help get business?'

Develop your sales sentences, especially opening statements and questions, by steadily working away at them. You should burnish them and your sales presentation as if they were a set of jewels. By doing this, you will acquire a natural, polished presentation and what is more, you will communicate more readily with prospects.

Make your telephone conversation sparkle

Your voice and choice of words do the selling on the telephone. Try to make them sparkle. Use words that stand out from the ordinary, that crystallize an idea in a phrase. You can achieve this with enthusiasm, practice, and zeal in increasing your vocabulary.

You must be interested in the occasional use of words that are out of the usual run of everyday speech, but not so out of touch that your listener needs a dictionary. Avoid using overworked words – they are dull and tired.

Do not use the same word, such as 'smashing', to describe everything. 'I had a smashing time on holiday.' 'It's a smashing film.' 'He's a smashing fellow.' 'That was a smashing meal.' Try being more descriptive and give the sentences a lift:

'I had an exhilarating holiday.'

'I had a very restful holiday.'

'I had a relaxing holiday.'

'It's a moving, tearful, penetrating, thoughtful, happy, enjoyable, unforgettable [or word that describes it in a more understandable way than "smashing"] film.'

'He's a kind, considerate person.'

'That was a memorable meal.'

Develop word command

Write down some of your sales sentences and then re-write them with other words. Use different sentences when you are talking. Here are a few statements about a software program supplied by a computer systems company:

'The program is very versatile.'

'The program is very flexible.'

'The program can be adapted to most uses.'

'You are not restricted to just the one use.'

83

'The program can be adapted to any use you need now or might do in the future.'

'Apart from accuracy, this program is probably the most versatile available today – in the US as well as the UK.'

'You cannot obtain a better program. Its versatility is unsur-passed.' [or 'cannot be beaten']

'You will only need this one program. It is so powerful and adaptable.'

Here's a car salesman telling a prospective customer about the amount of space in the boot:

'It's very roomy, especially the boot.'

'The boot's enormous.'

'You could put luggage and golf clubs for four in the boot.'

'It's the most spacious boot of any car in this class.'

'The boot is large enough to hold a picnic in it!'

'You could get lost in the boot!'

'The boot is ample for five adults on holiday.'

These are some of the ways in which the image of a large boot could be put across to the customer, getting away from the ordinary trite phrases we sometimes hear.

Comparatives and superlatives

Take care not to use too many superlatives in your conversation otherwise you will not be credible. If your product is the largest, the cheapest, the most comprehensive, and these are benefits for the customer, then say so, but in general, if you use comparatives rather than superlatives, your listener will be more inclined to accept the points you make in your sales presentation. For example, use the comparative 'larger' rather than the superlative, 'largest'; 'faster', not 'fastest'; tell the prospect that your product is one of the 'better' buys on the market rather than the 'best'. However, be careful not to reduce your sales presentation to an insipid, colourless tale. There is an obvious danger that by always using comparatives your conversation will sound lifeless and unenthusiastic.

The secret is to reserve the use of the superlative for your important selling sentences that contain the more, perhaps even the most, important product benefits.

If during a phone conversation, you have detected that the internal size of the product is critical and that the prospect wants the largest volume possible, then, if your product has the largest interior on the market, say so. Here, you would not use the comparative, you would use the superlative. This is yet another reason why you must listen carefully to the comments made by the prospect: so that you can use the appropriate sales sentences when they will do the most good. When using a superlative, have verbal evidence available to support it. If this support requires your showing or demonstrating the product then you would be unwise to develop your sales presentation on the phone. You should try for an appointment.

If, in fact, your product is the best buy, then make sure that you have evidence to back up the statement. If you were face to face with the prospect it would be a simple matter to have printed evidence from a recognized authority. On the phone, it is not so easy. Go over all your selling sentences and prune them of all the superlatives you cannot substantiate without some kind of visual aid.

Enthusiasm
You have to believe in what you are doing. You have to like what you are doing. Monday mornings should provide a new interest, a new challenge for you. There are many words of similar meaning that you can group with 'enthusiastic'. Eager, zealous, avid, lively, keen, fervent.

Increasing your vocabulary
Like everything else that is worth doing, you must practise the use of words and 'break them in', as you would a new pair of shoes. You will not be able to develop the skilful and accurate use of words overnight. Try to learn a new word, or more, every week. Find one that is unfamiliar to you in an article, newspaper or book. Look up its meaning and insert it in your diary for that day. It is easy to refresh your memory by looking back over the entries regularly.

The tools you use are words. While you should avoid using long complex words when short ones will do, you should take every opportunity of expanding your vocabulary. Some years ago, research was conducted on certain American university graduates prior to their graduation and, subsequently in their employment, some years after leaving university. There was a very high statistical correlation between the size of their salaries and the size of their vocabularies.

Diamond sparkles because of the different facets of its cut; your speech should sparkle because of the variety of living words you use. Express yourself in language that tells the prospect what the product looks like and what it will do for him.

Preparing a selling note sheet

First write down the attributes of the product. Consider each of these in turn and decide which are not only attributes but of benefit to the prospective customer. Understand that many will be of general benefit, and some will be of specific benefit to certain customers. The benefits have to be proven verbally, this is done with the aid of carefully worked out proof statements. Here is an example of proof statements being developed:

Attribute	*Benefit*	*Proof statement*
Compatible with CP/M.	Interchangeable with certain other equipment.	You are not restricted to just this one make.
		Most of our customers have it connected with other makes of equipment.
Reinforced centre drive.	1) Longer life. 2) Stability of operation.	*The disk will outlast ordinary disks.
		Some of our present customers have been using these disks for over five years and they have never had any trouble with them.
		Because of the reinforced centre drive, you never get a faulty drive such as 'flutter'.

*This is rejected as it only repeats what the benefit is – it doesn't sparkle!

Use of correct language

Words which are pronounced the same but spelt differently (homonyms) can be a barrier to effective communication. Take this conversation between a salesman and a boat-builder:

Salesman: I am sure this product will improve your sales.

Builder: Nonsense! The quality of our sails is known all over the world.

The confusion between 'sales' and 'sails' was eventually cleared up with amusement, and actually helped to promote a better relationship between the salesman and the boat-builder.

People give priority to the first meaning of a given word or sound. It never entered this salesman's mind that 'improving sales' could mean anything other than 'increasing turnover'. The customer reacted quickly to any suggestion that his 'sails' could be improved. Yet the salesman knew he was talking to a boat-builder and the boat-builder knew he was talking to a salesman. Each jumped to the conclusion that the meaning being conveyed was one he expected. This is one of the most important barriers to effective communication. Always be on your guard against it.

The difficulty increases when unusual words, or ordinary ones with unusual meanings, are used. Almost every trade, industry and profession has its special words or special meanings for common words.

The legal profession is a prime example of an occupational group that develops its own private language. Members of the profession grow so accustomed to using it that they tend to think it is normal. There is a good story of the aged and learned judge speaking severely to a lawyer in his court:

'Your client's evidence has been a waste of time. Surely he is familiar with the doctrine, *de minimis non curat lex*?'

The lawyer's rejoinder is also worth recording:

'My lord,' he replied, 'he talks of little else!'

The Latin phrase means that the law does not concern itself with very small matters.

The legal profession is not unique in this respect. Your own industry may have developed its private language which you may be using without realizing it: 'What about the LPHW job in Marlow. Has it been commissioned yet?' If you are in the heating and ventilation industry you will recognize this as a conversation about a low pressure hot water boiler, with the enquirer asking whether it is installed and working.

Control your voice and speech

If you are not already known to the prospect, your voice will be the first contact with the person at the other end of the line, and will convey an image to your listener. To project a pleasing personality you have to develop a pleasing, easy-to-understand voice and speech pattern.

Your voice is your transmitting tool. It takes two to communicate, but when you speak to someone, you are carrying out only one side of the activity – you are transmitting. For effective communication the other person has to receive correctly what you transmit. You must ensure, therefore, that your voice is in good condition and that you use words of the kind employed by the listener.

You certainly do not need to force your voice to deliver some sort of Shakespearian oration. You are not going on the stage and you do not have to project what you say to the back of the hall, but you do have to put over your messages so that they will be received by your listener as you intended.

When you sell on the phone, you need to transmit your messages in succinct, controllable passages, which requires breath control. Try sitting in a chair similar to the type you use when phoning, take a moderate breath, breathe out, pause, breathe in again moderately, then read aloud a passage from your daily newspaper. Consider how much you may sound like your favourite TV personality.

Articulation

It is good training to practise words that we do not often come across in ordinary, everyday reading. The reason is that you will often meet unusual customer names and names of products that have to be spoken clearly on the phone.

The most important word you will speak to a prospect is his name, and some names can be a little difficult to pronounce. Never be afraid to ask someone how they spell their name, if it sounds difficult. Even a common name such as Smith might be spelt Smythe. Make a note on your pad if there is a special way of saying that name.

You will appreciate that articulating words, that is, making the mouth and tongue work correctly so that the words mean something, is vitally important to you. Do not indulge in what is sometimes referred to as 'slurvian' – sloppy speech. Even ordinary words in an unusual setting often fail to make sense.

Read through the following carefully, understand what it is and then ask someone to listen while you say it clearly in a fairly brisk conversational speaking rate:

In mud eels are, in clay none.

In fir tar is, in oak none.

Ask them if they know what language it is. The answer is often 'Latin'. You can see it's English. Hearing it is a different matter.

Listen to yourself on a tape recorder. Give every syllable its true value. Make sure you sound the 't' in words such as water, butter, better. A number of people suppress the sound of 't' in their speech. This practice is called the glottal stop. It consists of cutting off air and throttling the 't' in the throat.

Avoid placing the sound of the letter 'l' on the ends of words such as 'idea', unless you really want to say 'ideal'. Make sure that any word that ends in 'ing' doesn't sound as though it ends in 'in'.

It is not only what you say to prospects but how you say it. And, how you say it means the sound, pitch and general articulation.

Self-examination questions on Chapter 11

11/1   What are the five points in the suggested plan for structuring your presentation?

11/2   Why is it necessary to make your sales presentation sparkle?

11/3   What should you not use too much of and why?

11/4   Why is controlling your voice important?

11/5   Of what use is 'slurvian'?

Chapter 12

How to Talk to People in Different Moods

The people you phone on business may often be unpredictable although, like people everywhere, the talkative person tends to keep the conversation going, while the taciturn one is usually quiet and ruminative.

Buyers cannot be put into different categories and dealt with by formulae. Be careful of over-classifying prospects into 'logical', 'bullying', or some other such category.

If you have already met the person whom you are going to phone, then you will know something of his or her personality. If not, you should be careful not to begin with a preconceived idea.

If you cultivate a pleasant, polite and helpful manner, the prospect should get a good impression from your voice. You too will get an idea of the kind of person to whom you are talking by hearing his voice and observing the speech pattern. Irrespective of the way in which we normally speak, our general well-being and health will often project a good mood or a bad one.

Talkative mood

You are not permitted to make your presentation. The prospect keeps talking and side-tracking you in all sorts of ways. It is very difficult to stem the flow of words. The way to deal with this mood is to *listen*. It may be costly, but you still have to listen, but positively. Listen for something that is said that you can link with your presentation. Negative listening is rather like lying on the beach with the tide coming in, and letting it wash backwards and forwards over you. Positive listening is more like running into the water and swimming. It is relating everything that is said to your presentation and when a point registers, trying to get in and say 'Ah!', and put your point. If you cannot put your proposal forward because the prospect is in full flood, remember to jot down notes of points as they are made on your pad. Sooner or later the prospect will pause. You can then say, 'Ah! Mr Prospect, with regard to [point number one], and [point number two],' and so on.

Talkative moods are often possessed by what are called 'detail men'. They don't so much tell you points or results, they tell you in minute detail all the ins and outs. This is their pleasure. You can often develop a first-class relationship with people who want to talk by putting in the appropriate closed question and open probe (see Chapter 6) to stimulate and maintain their flow.

The reason for all the talking is that the prospect has not yet appreciated the strength and value of your proposal. Until you get the chance to tell him, he never will!

Talkative moods may also be the result of the prospect being excited or enthusiastic about something that has happened. You must listen and try to find out if this is the reason; you may be able to use this to put your proposition in a favourable light.

Silent mood

The opposite of the talkative person is the prospect who, for reasons best known to himself, is rather silent. It is as though his thoughts are far away.

You must always be alert to this mood because it can signal some serious happening in the prospect's private life. He may have just received a most painful telephone call about the health of someone in his family and be about to make up his mind to leave the office. He is unlikely to tell you all; it depends on his general character and how well you know him. However, he may not wish to talk with or listen to you.

If you consider the prospect is unusually silent, or apparently reluctant to respond, put an open probe and listen carefully to the answer. You cannot remain on the phone for too long with both of you saying nothing. If your open probe doesn't work, try one or two closed questions. If you get a response, then use an open probe to obtain more information.

Happy mood

It's always more pleasant to talk to someone who is obviously cheerful. You must be careful to reflect the mood and sound pleased with life yourself. Even if you yourself have something to be unhappy about, you must not disclose this to the prospect. Few things can be more disturbing and annoying when we are in a happy mood than for someone to come on the phone and start being miserable.

If your respondent is in a happy mood, then be happy for him or her; take advantage of the situation and aim to achieve the objective of phoning.

Miserable mood

From time to time you will phone someone who is very miserable. Generally, you should avoid getting involved or spending too much time here because, unless you have something that will counteract the reason for the mood, you will get nowhere. If you know the person, then you might use carefully constructed probes to find out the reason but, in the main, it is better to curtail the conversation and phone again.

Indecisive mood

How often are we undecided! We are confronted with a good menu in a restaurant and we cannot make up our mind which of two equally attractive dishes to have. We are confronted in a shop with, say, two shirts, and we cannot make up our mind which to have.

The prospect who is in an indecisive mood will say, 'I'll have a word with my colleague', 'I'll consult my solicitor', 'I'll definitely have it later on'.

If the indecision is with, say, the prospect's secretary, and she is not certain whether or not to make an appointment for her boss, then you must make the decision for her:

> 'I appreciate your problem, Miss Smith, that you're not sure of his movements. I'll risk being disappointed and make it, say, 10.30 on Tuesday morning as that's the time you have nothing in his diary. If I call and he can't see me, that's my bad luck.'

> 'I understand your difficulty but, I'll tell you what. We'll make it, say, 10.30 on Tuesday and, if he can't, then perhaps you'd be kind enough to give me a ring.'

When you have to make decisions directly for prospects, you can do this and tell them things can always be altered later if necessary.

Aggressive mood

If you know the respondent, you will know whether or not this is the usual mood and will be able to deal with it accordingly. If you do not know the person, then be careful of mistaking what you think is aggressiveness for briskness and a desire to get on with things. If you are normally a quiet, slow-to-act personality, then anyone with a normally brisk manner will appear to you as aggressive. So, be careful of misinterpreting the situation.

People you have not previously met or spoken with and who sound very aggressive on the phone should be treated as you would a sergeant-major if you were a recruit! He shouts: 'Attention!' and you should jump to attention. He fires at you: 'When can I have your reply?' and you say: 'The day after tomorrow.'

Whatever questions or commands you get, respond crisply and avoid starting your reply with, 'Well ...'. If the person is normally aggressive, or sounds aggressive, then he or she will respect short, crisp replies and will not take kindly to long, slow answers.

Over-friendly mood

Someone in this mood will agree with everything you say and be extremely hard to tie down. He will call you by your first name and promise things that lead you to think that nothing will ever materialise.

You must take a fairly firm line with such a prospect and ask him if he understands exactly what is being agreed to. Put all the proposals into monetary terms. That usually has the over-friendly type listening and talking more seriously.

Self-examination questions on Chapter 12

12/1 Is it recommended that, generally, you should reflect the customers' moods?

12/2 What is best to use when dealing with customers on the phone, closed questions or open probes?

12/3 You are talking with a customer who is normally pleasant but now sounds miserable. How would you deal with the call?

Chapter 13

How to Handle Complaints

Treat a customer complaint as you would treat a medical emergency. Give it priority. Regard it as you would a patient with cardiac arrest. Immediate rapid attention is essential. This means that you must have an 'emergency kit' to hand. It's no use treating a customer with a complaint as a normal customer. You cannot give him the slightest excuse for further complaint.

The emergency kit

This should be the procedure which is adopted by you and all other people in the organization, to placate the complainant and convince him or her that the best treatment possible is being given. Do not respond by saying, 'Just a moment sir [or madam] I'll get one of our complaint forms. ... Now, your name is ...?'

If your organization uses complaint forms, always have them readily available. Keep them as you would a first-aid kit, just in case you ever need them! When a complainant comes on the phone and starts outlining the problems, pull out your special form and start filling it in.

Don't take the complainant through the form asking this question and that question, putting this point and that one. *Listen* and enter remarks and points in the appropriate spaces as he or she is speaking. As you listen make sure you get the name, telephone number and address. If you have to listen to a long list of angry comments leave it until the first few blasts from the customer have died away before you ask for name, address etc.

You can quench the fire of the complainant's anger if you have an early opportunity of saying, 'What is your telephone number, sir? ... extension, and your name? ... [repeat it to make sure you've got it correctly] Right, let *me* call you back.'

He may say 'No', and continue the conversation, but that's fine, you've made the offer. If he accepts, phone the complainant back straight away; *do not delay*.

No matter how aggressive the complainant, respond with politeness. Even if the person on the phone is rude and offensive, do not react in the same manner. There is nothing like a calm, understanding and utterly polite manner to defuse an irate customer. Do not take it personally, but, do *listen*!

Complainant:	Hullo! Hullo! I'd like to speak to your managing director.
You:	Yes, sir. May I tell him who is calling?
Complainant:	My name is Fuller.
You:	Right, Mr Fuller. And may I tell him the nature of your enquiry?
Complainant:	Yes. We've got one of your word processing systems and we have never experienced such difficulties. The thing is absolutely useless. It was delivered last week and we simply haven't been able to get it going. You trained one of our staff for a day, but she can't make it work properly. Every time I phone your service department we get different advice. I'm absolutely fed up with the whole thing. It's disgraceful that a company with your reputation should treat a customer like this.
You:	Mr Fuller. Please, let me phone you back immediately. You shouldn't be paying for this call. What is your number, sir?
Complainant:	Oh! It doesn't matter.
You:	Please, sir. I think we should be calling you. You must let me phone you back. Do you have an extension number?
Complainant:	No! It's all right. The cost of the call is not important. What is important is that we were going to rely on this system so much and we are in an absolutely chaotic state. Yesterday ...

Let the customer go on. Don't interrupt. Listen. Offer to phone back again as soon as you have the opportunity. If the customer declines, at least you will have made the offer and that will help to cool the situation a little. Continue to listen, making appropriate notes on paper, but preferably on any special complaints form your company uses.

When the complainant has run out of steam and has said as much as he feels necessary, then go into the company routine for providing service:

You:	Mr Fuller, you've obviously had a lot of trouble. I'm sorry about that. I'm going to put you through to our Mr Roberts. He's not actually the managing director but he has the authority to sort out your problem to your complete satisfaction. Please speak with him first of all,

sir. If you're not satisfied with what he suggests, he will put you back to me and I will connect you immediately with Mr James, the managing director. If I put you through to Mr James first, he would want to know why your problem couldn't be solved by Mr Roberts and this would delay our service to you.

This emergency kit – company procedure for dealing with complaints on the phone – will need to be updated from time to time, especially if the company has many different types of products.

Avoid devising a complaints form that covers every product and service. As it is unlikely to be used very often, the form must be easily understood and used by the person who has to fill it in. It is better to have a form in a colour unique from every other form in the business with spaces for the absolute essentials – name, initials, company, address, telephone number, date, time, nature of complaint, who is going to take action to deal with it, what the complainant has been told.

If you should pick up the phone and hear an enraged customer on the other end, always talk to them, even though it's nothing to do with you or your department. Ask questions. Because it is nothing to do with you, you will need to find out a lot more than normal about it. Make sure that the customer knows what you are doing, and deal with the complaint in as complete a manner as possible.

Tell the customer that you will start things moving, that it will be handled by someone else. If you know who will handle the complaint, tell the customer; if you don't know, tell him or her that you will phone back and say who will be dealing with it and when. Give your name and telephone extension clearly so that the complainant is put at ease and can contact you should the need arise. Express your regret that the person has had to phone to complain but never agree that it is justified. Even though it sounds as though there is a genuine complaint, obvious from the facts as stated by the customer, you are only hearing one side. Always pass the complaint to the person or department who deal with it. After all, you haven't heard the company side yet! It is not unknown for false complaints to be made in the hope that some extra service can be extracted!

Checklist for handling complaints

1. Listen and take notes, without commenting. If you have a company complaint form, ensure you always have one or

two at hand by the phone. Hear the complainant out, completely.

2. Sympathize with the fact that the person has had to phone but *do not* apologize because the complaint has not been investigated. Fault has not been established and it is not unknown for customers to 'try it on'.

3. Establish the name, address and phone number of complainant, record the date and time of call.

4. Establish the facts and repeat them so that the complaint agrees with what you are recording.

5. Decide or find out who has the knowledge and authority to deal with the complaint and can make a decision to put it right.

6. Decide on the best course of action.

7. Obtain the customer's approval on the proposed course of action.

8. Take that action.

9. Make a copy of the details. Follow up.

10. Learn from the experience for future avoidance if this is possible.

Self-examination questions on Chapter 13

13/1 What is recommended as one good method of quenching the fire of a complainant's anger as soon as he is on the phone to you?

13/2 What three main things do you have to do when listening to a complaint from a customer on the phone?

13/3 If your company has a complaints form, how would you use it if a customer came on the phone with a complaint?

13/4 Under what conditions would you agree with the customer that a complaint is justified?

Chapter 14

How to Find Customers

The telephone is a very important means by which to find out whether or not a sales lead is worth following up with a face-to-face call. In this way, it contributes greatly to finding customers. This process is called 'qualifying the sales leads'.

The three factors

To determine whether or not a lead might become a customer, three key factors have to be established:

- Is there a budget to purchase the product about which the telephone call is being made?
- When is the purchase to be made – immediately, in three months, six months or a year or more?
- Who is or, more likely, are the main people who will decide on the purchase?

The first factor will be related to the size and value of the sale of a typical product and will quickly establish whether the person on the other end of the line is aware of the cost of the product. Many companies would like to acquire products that are being advertised on the market, but do not have the means with which to acquire them. A computer would doubtless be of immense value to many organizations, but often intending buyers are not aware of the cost involved.

Some people believe it a good idea to have a word processor; it would speed up their letters, reports, quotations and also prove invaluable for 'personalized' letters with individual names automatically typed in the appropriate places.

Many companies announce in their advertising that their low-priced computers include accounting, record-keeping and word processing software. The image created is of a computer that will do all the desired things for a price of a few hundred pounds. This is not so and creates a difficulty for suppliers.

The company that is selling professional word processing

equipment for between five and ten times the price and is seeking prospects on the phone must quickly determine whether the prospective customer knows what it will cost and whether there is an adequate budget for the equipment.

The second factor – the timing of the purchase – is important once you have established that the prospective customer knows the likely cost and that funds have been earmarked for the purchase. Companies who are currently thinking seriously about obtaining such a product are red-hot prospects. They must be regarded in a different light from those who will be considering the acquisition of such a product 'during the next financial year'.

The third factor is to find out to whom you have to put your proposition. While it is important to pay due regard to the person with whom the initial phone call is being made, it is vital to find out who will influence the purchasing decision. If the proposed purchase is for capital equipment, several people will be involved in the placing of the order. It will be normal for the proposed acquisition to be discussed at production management meetings, budget meetings and board meetings. The decision will not be made by one person but will be the result of many opinions being sought.

If you are selling capital goods, you will need to develop wide contacts in the prospective customer's organization. The first person you speak with on the phone will obviously be able to help, but that is only the start; you will need to expand your contacts within the company after you have visited them.

Similarly, if you are selling consumer products in bulk to a large chain of department stores, it is likely that you will be negotiating long-term contracts. But, it is unlikely that there is just one person involved in the purchasing decision and you must find out who influences the buying decision. Even the most important buyers in a department store have assistant buyers with whom they discuss movement of stock.

Using the telephone to find customers

Saleswoman: Good afternoon. My name's Johnson of Smith Limited. We supply a number of customers in the north similar in size to yours, with a range of speciality foods. Can you help me please? Do you stock a wide range of foods?

Operator: Yes, we do. We have a large food hall.

Saleswoman: Is it possible to have a word with the buyer this afternoon? And, may I have the name?

Operator: I'll put you through to the department. Hold the line. ...

Unknown:	Afternoon.
Saleswoman:	Good afternoon. My name's Liz Johnson of Smith Limited. We supply speciality foods mainly to the north of England and Scotland but we're expanding south. You stock various foods of course?
Unknown:	Yes, we do.
Saleswoman:	When do you normally purchase?
Unknown:	Depends. Daily, weekly, monthly ...
Saleswoman:	I see. Who should I try to see to discuss this?
Unknown:	Who did you say you are?
Saleswoman:	Smith Limited of Banff. My name's Johnson – Liz Johnson. And you're mister ...?
Perry:	Perry – Frank Perry.
Saleswoman:	Well, Mr Perry, whom would you suggest I see?
Perry:	Well, you wouldn't want to see me. I don't buy foodstuffs. You'll need to see ...

And so on. Ask closed questions and open probes to find out if they stock, when they buy and who to see (see Chapter 6).

Decision-making unit

In every company there is usually a group of people who influence the purchase and source of supplies. Sometimes this is on a formal basis; often, it is an informal collection of people. Such groups are called decision-making units, DMUs.

These DMUs are frequently involved in the construction of a procedure called vendor performance evaluation, or supplier performance evaluation.

Your product may be the highest priced on the market because your quality is the best and you can deliver the next day. This does not mean that you will get the business. From working with many different companies we have found that the main criteria for a buying decision are:

- Price
- Reliability of supplier
- Ease of getting emergency supplies
- Service
- Quality
- Uniqueness of the product

- Accessibility of representatives of the supplier
- Delivery.

These are not listed in order of importance but for the initial letters to spell the mnemonic, PRESQUAD, a word that makes it easy to remember. A weighted points method of evaluating suppliers is illustrated with these eight criteria:

Criteria	Weight*	Rating†	W × R
Price	10		
Reliability	6		
Emergency supplies	4		
Service	6		
Quality	10		
Uniqueness of product	3		
Accessibility of people	4		
Delivery	7		

*Weights are usually decided by a committee or by reference to various department heads (or members of the decision-making unit) and applied to all suppliers and potential suppliers. In a large organization there might be many pages of criteria.

† A rating is applied to individual suppliers.

Each weight and rating has a maximum (in this simplified example it is 10 for each) and the weights are made to sum to a convenient number. In this example, you can see that it is 50, so that the maximum W × R total is 500.

When you have the opportunity you should find out from some of your very good customers whether they have a supplier performance evaluation procedure and, if so, how your company scores. The good points you will be able to use in subsequent sales presentations to prospects.

The problem when putting propositions for capital goods and purchases that require a large outlay of funds, is how to find the answers to the three key factors: Is there a budget? When will the purchase be made? Who decides? You need to work to a semi-structured questionnaire. This means that you will have prepared all the attributes, benefits and proof statements about your product, and will have opening questions and statements written down so that you can refer to them.

Assumptive questioning technique

This is putting questions in the form of assumed answers. Here are some examples:

'There will be more than one person involved in this decision?'

'You normally place your contract at this time of the year?'

'You would need two work stations?'

'It would have to be capable of graphics as well?'

'Your budget is limited to £100,000?'

'You know the properties of expanded polystyrene?'

'You stock all sizes?'

'There are others in your company who should see the demonstration?'

'It will need to be in excess of five kilowatts?'

The prospect on the other end of the phone will either agree or will correct your question/statement.

Every newspaper, especially the local ones, all the trade, technical and professional journals are sources of leads for prospective customers. Scan the appointments vacant columns for vacancies relevant to the business you are in. The fact that a company is advertising for a data processing manager, a supervisor for an extended plant, another draughtsman, and so on may be relevant to your products. You will save a lot of time and expense by finding out on the phone if the suspect could be a prospect.

A visit to your local reference library is worthwhile. The librarian should be able to supply you with a great many sources of likely customers.

Combining a telesales approach with a direct mail operation is a way to find customers. You might mail the list of prospects then telephone every one, irrespective of whether or not there has been a response. You can phone and send the literature after the phone call. You can mail a series of shots and phone, and so on.

One company that markets building and construction equipment and tools makes great use of the phone in qualifying leads, and they concentrate on local authorities. The following criteria are used:

- What type of machinery and equipment is the organization using and has it been using any equipment similar to the products of the enquiring company?

- Has a budget been set for the next purchasing period?

- Who is responsible for approving suppliers and authorizing purchase decisions of such equipment?
- Where are these people based?
- Make an appointment for a visit with the red-hot prospects and send literature to the others.

Of the appointments made, more than 70 per cent eventually place orders with the company.

Self-examination questions on Chapter 14

14/1 What format is suggested for use on the phone to decide who are potential prospects?

14/2 When looking for customers, how do you select those you think you ought to phone?

14/3 What is the first thing to establish when qualifying a sales lead on the phone?

14/4 What are the second and third things that have to be established to qualify a sales lead?

Chapter 15

How to Arouse the Buying Inclination

Here we are concerned with the 'buying' inclination but this is not strictly limited to the buying of a product or service. It also includes 'buying' the idea of agreeing to an appointment.

Who makes the decision?

The most simple situation is where you are phoning a one-man company. That man makes the decisions. You phone him; tell him who you are; explain your proposition; and there is nobody else you have to worry about in order to get a decision. Easy! Or is it?

Does he make the decision on his own? Is he influenced by no one at all? Does he simply decide to acquire a new piece of machinery and that is his decision and his alone? Or does he take advice? Most likely he will have discussed it with people he knows, people in a similar business. Probably with his accountant, who will advise him on the advisability of such an acquisition at that time.

However, if it is a decision to buy a new diary for next year, a new set of filing equipment, a new desk calculator, a new type of phone, he is unlikely to take too much counsel from other people. Even with such small purchases, however, he will have been influenced by what he has seen in other offices and factories, what he has seen in journals and newspapers, what he has heard from others. In other words, his decision will have been the result of a number of influences.

Consider his proposed buying of a calculator to replace the one he has been using for many years but that is now broken. If he meets a person using something which looks neat, easy to see and easy to manipulate and asks an opinion of the owner, the reply is likely to influence his purchase. He will ask two questions: 'Where did you get it?' and 'What did you pay?'

An enthusiastic response from the owner will have a great effect. 'It's all right, but I find it very difficult to operate', will also have an effect, but the opposite one. The owner of the calculator may not be capable of handling it; his problems may be entirely due to operator inefficiency. Nevertheless, the reply will have conditioned the inquirer.

The more enthusiastic and sincere are the comments made to us, the more we are inclined to accept them at face value, so it follows that, to arouse the buying inclination in people, we must really believe in what we are doing and talk about it with genuine enthusiasm (see Chapter 11).

In many companies, the acquiring of operating materials and supplies is according to specification. When you phone to try and make an appointment to put your case, you will realize that you have no chance immediately of selling anything other than yourself and your company to that person on the phone.

Buying an appointment

If you have not been supplying them previously, you have to find out whether there is a specification and, if there is, whether your company can be given the opportunity of quoting to it. At best, you have to stimulate the inclination in the prospect to 'buy' an appointment with you; at least, you have to sell the idea of sending him some literature. You can readily appreciate that, to progress such a situation to a buying situation, you need to have carefully prepared stages, of which a face-to-face appointment is definitely one.

In addition to buying such operating materials and supplies, companies purchase capital equipment and important services such as those of consultants or advertising agencies. In these large, one-off acquisitions, the main board will decide. If the purchase is really a very important one, then the board will want to hear presentations themselves from the intending suppliers. If the purchase is not so large, they will very likely arrive at a decision based on the facts laid before them by their managers, and on their managers' opinions.

You should begin to see that, whatever the purchase, it is possible for your enthusiasm, knowledge and general manner to show through, whether it is in a face-to-face situation or by the medium of words on paper, or words in ears!

The buying decision

Every DMU will be a unique combination of individuals with varying degrees of influence in different product areas. If you fail to direct sufficient effort towards sifting out who are the people whose opinions truly matter you could, without realizing it, be spending a lot of time on someone who has only moderate influence and is not a key decision maker.

Also bear in mind that departmental responsibilities may overlap considerably. For example, buyers may have an influence on the purchase of raw materials; transport managers on vehicles; engineering managers on production equipment, and so on.

If there is one person who is acknowledged to take decisions in a company, he is still influenced by people in the organization and, if you win their support, you will gain his support through their efforts. Thus, you must ignore no one. You cannot prejudge any situation and decide that any particular people are, or are not, important to your quest.

Buying decisions by professional buyers are seldom entirely rational. Though most of them would argue against this, you will understand that human beings can only act and react on emotions. Every buyer is subject to irrational and emotional influences and it is these that are so hard to isolate. Mainly, buyers seek security from their company's suppliers. They make 'establishment' decisions, that is, they do not venture too far from the norm when making buying decisions and tend to stick with the long-standing supplier who is generally accepted by others in the company.

Even if a new, smaller company offers a product that is better quality and lower in price, the large, well-established supplier has an advantage that arises out of this emotional element in the purchasing decision.

Ask any important appointed dealer about his supplying company's products and you will learn that they are the best on the market. The best design, quality and price. If this were true, that supplying company would have the major share of the market, which is not always so.

The reason is the considerable depth of the relationship existing between the supplying company and the dealer. An expenses-paid visit to the supplying company's headquarters as their guest will make a very strong impression on the dealer. The whole package of appointed-dealer 'goodies' has the effect of distorting the rational buying process. The emotional content is high. And, when the dealer sells to customers in his store, the engendered exuberance is transmitted to the customer.

To arouse the buying inclination, develop empathy with the prospect and never forget the power of enthusiasm. It has the capacity of breaking down many barriers to buying.

Drives that stimulate action

The main drives suggested by a well-known sociologist, A H Maslow, are the following five needs:

- Basic needs
- Security
- Gregariousness, or belonging
- Status
- Self-fulfilment.

Without going into these in great detail it is fairly easy to see that all of us have the first one – basic needs. When you are selling on the telephone (or anywhere else for that matter), you must decide where in the hierarchy of needs your type of product is placed by the respondent. Some products which are considered as almost essential by one respondent may be viewed as a luxury by another respondent.

Security needs – perhaps the desire to hold on to our job and position – vary from person to person. This is why many respondents will stay with the supplier they know rather than risk going elsewhere. They don't want to endanger their position in the company.

The need to belong to a group, the desire to be accepted by others in that group, can be very strong motivating factors. Your prospect on the phone may be impressed by the fact that, by dealing with you and your company, it places him in a group to which he aspires.

Status needs are those which drive people to improve and increase their own importance in the eyes of their family, their employers and others. These needs often stimulate them to acquire things which can be regarded as possessing a high status and generally provide an outward show of their importance. If you think of how much the average executive is concerned with the make and model of car supplied by the company, you will understand how personal and powerful is this question of status. Always talk to a respondent as though he or she is important. In fact, all customers are important and there is everything to gain by letting them know this. Even flattery helps!

'Ah! My favourite customer, Mr Jones! I trust you are well?'

'Hullo, Mr Muir. Always nice to talk with one of my shrewder customers. Business is fair I hope?'

'As I've always said, Miss Brodie, if I can get you to stock our new lines when we introduce them, they must be good. You have a reputation for keen buying.'

Don't overdo it! Just little touches here and there used like herbs and seasoning in cooking – with discretion. These complimentary comments will probably be remembered. Aim to make your respondents feel good.

Self-fulfilment needs are the desire to 'do one's own thing', to realize an ambition, to achieve a certain position, to have a degree of power, and so on.

You cannot arouse the buying inclination until you know what motivates the person on the other end of the phone. Therefore you must question the prospect appropriately and *listen* to the replies.

Telephoning the 'company' man

It is easier to understand the motivation when phoning a prospect employed within a large company. The employee probably works within rules, procedures and specifications, but has emotions. You have to communicate the understanding that he will not compromise his position one iota by agreeing to see you. You have to develop openings and further statements that prove you have the knowledge so that they appeal to his reasoning as well as his feelings.

Make sure that you have a sound reason for suggesting anything. If you are trying to close with an appointment, make sure that the prospect is given a reason for seeing you.

Where appropriate you must create three things in the mind of the prospect:

- Curiosity
- Involvement
- Confidence

Curiosity is a strong motivator and, when you involve the respondent's company, it is very powerful. You arouse curiosity by being different from all other sales people on the phone with your knowledge of your product, the professional way in which you conduct the phone conversation and, above all, by your cheerful manner and keenness.

Have an objective for every phone call. Keep this in mind as you speak and listen. Know what you are going to say before you pick up the phone and, as soon as you have opened the conversation, know what you are going to say in response to the replies. Prepare important openings, sales sentences and benefit statements and have them in easy-to-read format in front of you when you are on the phone. You will soon learn to say them without needing to refer to them too often.

Involve the respondent and his company by always expressing sincere interest in her or him and the company. Don't try to sell to the respondent but help him or her to buy. Answer questions quickly and truthfully but don't volunteer information that is not asked for unless it progresses your presentation. Don't confuse issues; stick to the point under discussion. Make it easy for the respondent to make a decision.

A clear, lucid and simple presentation that is free from jargon will gradually create confidence in the respondent.

Self-examination questions on Chapter 15

15/1   Why do you think you should commit your sales pitch to paper before making a phone call?

15/2   Can flattery have any value on the phone?

15/3   What three things should you aim to achieve when opening a sales conversation?

Appendices

Checklist for Use after a Telephone Call

Copy this list and use it for your initial calls. Not every point will be of relevance to your work, but gradually you will develop a trained method of conducting your telephone sales activities, designed to achieve results. A specimen phone call record sheet is supplied on page 114 you can use this as a model and eventually draw one up that is appropriate to your particular operation. Make it simple. Don't keep records for the sake of it. Make them work for the future.

CHECKLIST FOR PHONE CALLS

Did you have pad ready?	[ ]
Did you have pen/ballpoint/pencil (and spare)?	[ ]
Timepiece?	[ ]
Diary – open at current dates?	[ ]
Script of openings, statements, product benefits?	[ ]
Note date and time of call?	[ ]
Note length of time of call?	[ ]
Did you get name, spelling? Initials?	[ ]
Address?	[ ]
Position in company?	[ ]
Telephone number, extension?	[ ]
Best time to call?	[ ]
Did they know who was calling?	[ ]
Your name?	[ ]
Who your company is?	[ ]
Why you were phoning?	[ ]
Did you have a main/initial objective for phoning?	[ ]
Were prospect's needs identified?	[ ]
Did prospect understand/agree needs?	[ ]
Did you make an offer?	[ ]
Did you achieve initial/main objective?	[ ]
Do you know who authorizes purchases?	[ ]
Make notes during conversation?	[ ]
Were any product benefits related to needs?	[ ]
If appointment, entered in diary?	[ ]
If order, quotation, letter, action initiated?	[ ]

Specimen Phone Call Record Sheet

Company _____

Address _____

_____

Telephone No. _____ Date 1st Call _____

Best time/day to phone _____

1st Contact _____ Initials _____

Position _____

Prospect's Activities _____

_____

Possible Products _____

Names, Titles of Influencers/Decision Makers _____

_____

_____

_____

Notes:

Action Plan

1. Prepare list of product benefits.
2. Alongside each benefit leave room for insertion of proof statements.
3. Obtain list of possible contacts, with phone numbers.
4. Start a phone script book with opening statements, opening questions, follow-up remarks, short descriptions of product/service, proof statements, dealing with objections, reasons why prospect should agree to see you, buy from you.
5. Have pad, writing instruments, diary, watch ready.
6. Insert date and time on page of pad.
7. Write down first phone number and name of prospect.
8. Make note of initial objective (to get an appointment, to send literature to named person, to sell product etc)
9. Write down opening to be used with telephone operator, receptionist or secretary.
10. Phone, start talking and *listening*, making notes on pad.

Answers to Self-examination Questions

1/1   Considering all the possible good points that can emerge from any situation.

1/2   Make an appointment to see that prospect when you are next in the area, bid him (or her) well, in a pleasant manner and quickly look for the next prospective customer.

1/3   Be interesting and enthusiastic in what you say and how you say it. Adopt a positive attitude in thought and word.

1/4   Always be prepared and when you meet an opportunity, use that preparation.

2/1   Let the respondent know as quickly as necessary in your presentation that you are selling.

2/2   Because you often have to get past the receptionist and the secretary before you can meet the prospect.

2/3   Just make more telephone calls.

3/1   Because otherwise your conversation with the prospect is likely to be disjointed.

3/2   Get to the point as quickly as you can when you start a conversation with a respondent. Give your name and the name of your company. Summarize the point of your call in the first sentence.

3/3   As soon as the real needs are understood.

4/1   Usually the after-dinner speaker has been previously announced to the people attending the dinner and they are looking forward to hearing the speech. Also, the speaker is not interrupted.

4/2   When speaking face to face with a prospect you can be seen and appraised. If you have a product with you, it can be seen. On the phone you have only your voice to help you.

4/3   Immediately after you have said your 'Good morning', etc, and told the prospect about your company and the product you are hoping to sell.

5/1   Because you are never sure what the prospect might say in response.

5/2   Actively listening to what the prospective customer says to you.

5/3   Because a good opening is the beginning of the sales presentation.

6/1   Because it is restricted to you and the listener.

6/2   One that will be answered by a single word, or as few words as necessary.

6/3   A question that invites the respondent to expand with more information.

6/4   Identify the real need. This means you must develop your sales presentation using open probes and closed questions as appropriate to reveal this need. Make sure that the prospect understands what it is, and then appreciates how your offer will satisfy that need.

7/1   Because if he does not, he is not going to be receptive to your offer.

7/2   You have to listen carefully to what the prospect is saying so that you are able to select from what is said and use this information to build barriers.

7/3   You must prepare a list of product benefits and, preferably, proof statements that support those benefits, because it is no use simply stating the benefit. You have to prove it to the listener by the supporting statement you make.

7/4   Only after you have identified it, made sure that the prospect understands it, and have explicitly mentioned it.

8/1   Until you have identified the need or needs, actually said it in words, and the prospect has understood, agreed and resolved either explicitly or implicitly to satisfy the need or needs.

8/2   You should not agree, because losing orders, or perhaps, more accurately, not getting orders, is not simply because you have not closed properly. The prospect may not be able to afford it, may be assessing a number of other offers, may be under instructions to place business with another organization, and many other reasons.

8/3   Not shutting up when the prospect is ready to give the order, or not agreeing the objective you set yourself before you picked up the phone. It means that the salesperson goes on talking and not listening.

9/1　You may have answered this question 'Yes' or 'No'. I think that you should always be prepared to help the prospect to assess the proposition because this will ensure that you have covered your ground very thoroughly and know the advantages of your offer.

9/2　A price that is acceptable to you there and then while you are talking on the phone; a price that is quite high, but lower than you can accept; a ridiculously low price.

9/3　Anywhere, but perhaps most likely when you arrive at the price.

9/4　To avoid them arising in the first place. If this is not always possible, respond to them immediately they are raised and keep a record of them and how you dealt with them.

10/1　Yes!

10/2　Remain silent!

10/3　Listen intently to what they say, and how they say it.

10/4　Because you will impress them on the mind of your listener.

11/1　Opening the sale; finding out the real need and getting the prospect to understand it and agree with it; getting the prospect to resolve to satisfy that need; making the offer; helping the prospect to assess your offer; obtaining the decision.

11/2　If your voice sounds as though you are pleasant and helpful, and the way you express yourself is interesting, the prospect is more likely to listen to you and your proposition.

11/3　You should not use too many superlatives or you will not be credible.

11/4　Because your respondent has to receive correctly what you transmit.

11/5　'Slurvian' is slovenly speech. It has no use at all.

12/1　If a customer, well known to you or not, tells you he has had a poor holiday, while you might sympathize, you should be very careful not to become involved in being associated with her or his recent experience. Remember that the customer was responsible for selecting the holiday and anything you say that is critical of the country, town or hotel where the holiday was spent is, in a way, denigrating the customer's choice. It is better simply to listen and let the customer 'run out of steam' and tell you all the problems. As soon as the 'complaint' has been aired you can say something along the lines of, 'Well let's talk about something more pleasant,' and introduce the subject of your phone call.

12/2   Both! You must listen and use open probes or closed questions depending on what you hear.

12/3   Avoid being gay and light-hearted. The respondent may have serious problems.

13/1   Ask for the complainant's telephone number and offer to phone back immediately.

13/2   Give the call priority; listen completely to the complaint and do not interrupt but jot down notes on your pad; tell the complainant what you propose to do.

13/3   Use a company complaint form as the complainant gives you the information, but enter the details as the complainant is talking. If there are any vital points not covered such as address, telephone number, put these questions at the end.

13/4   Never agree with a complainant that a complaint is justified.

14/1   You need to find out whether the company uses a product or service similar to the one you are offering; do they have a budget for purchasing or does the prospect know the likely cost; who is responsible for buying?

14/2   Don't prejudge. Phone 'every shop in the village'!

14/3   In general, who the best people are to talk to about the matter.

14/4   There are three main things: Is there a budget? When is the purchase to be made? Who makes the decision to purchase? The order in which you search for these data will depend on your type of product.

15/1   Because you must practise them to give them the right amount of emphasis and meaning. If they are written down you will be more able to say them correctly and subsequently modify them in the light of experience.

15/2   Used carefully and judiciously, it always has a good effect.

15/3   Raise the curiosity of the listener; get the listener involved; create confidence.

Appendix 5

Objectivity Test

If you want to use the telephone successfully in business you will need to practise and train yourself. This test has been constructed in a manner that will probe and examine what you know and how that knowledge should be applied.

If you have studied the book diligently you should obtain a score in excess of 50 per cent.

If you achieve a score of 80 per cent or more, you have done very well and may consider yourself as well informed and skilled in selling in general, and in telephone selling in particular.

If you achieve between 35–50 per cent you should revise appropriate parts of the book.

If your attempt scores below 35 per cent you need to reread the book carefully.

The six blocks, U, V, W, X, Y and Z, each contain statements or questions, some of which are relatively easy and others more difficult. Each statement or question has several possible responses, not all of which are true, correct or valid. You respond to the statements/questions by selecting one, two, three, four, five or, sometimes, none of the responses.

The answers are given on page 130.

Block U

U 1 The book:
- (a) Is about telephone selling.
- (b) Is about selling.
- (c) Is about selling telephones.
- (d) Is about selling using the telephone.
- (e) Is about selling but only using the telephone.

U 2 When selling by phone:
- (a) You are always at an advantage.
- (b) You are always at a disadvantage.
- (c) You are never at an advantage.
- (d) You are never at a disadvantage.
- (e) You have an advantage and a disadvantage.

U 3 Which of the following statements do you consider are true

according to the book?
- (a) You can gain an insight into a prospect's body language by listening.
- (b) A phone call is always a disturbance.
- (c) Because talker and listener are discussing together on the phone, they are in similar environments.
- (d) All figures should be stated in universal metric.
- (e) Selling by phone is completely different from other forms of selling.

U 4 What use are you recommended to make of a prospect's secretary when you contact their company?
- (a) She is the one who can really influence the placing of the order.
- (b) To establish the most convenient time to call on the prospect.
- (c) To ascertain the structure of the organization.
- (d) To make an appointment to call on the prospect.
- (e) To obtain the right 'key' to approach the prospect.

U 5 If you wish to talk personally with a prospect in an organization:
- (a) Use any device, because selling means getting hold of the one person who can place the order.
- (b) Don't waste time talking with other people.
- (c) Tell the operator who you are and say, 'Tell Mr Prospect that [John Smith] is on the phone please.'
- (d) Don't waste time explaining your business with the telephone operator.
- (e) Any reasonable subterfuge should be used as long as you have a good sales presentation to make when you eventually talk to the prospect.

Block V
V 1 After reading the relevant parts of the book, with which of the following do you agree?
- (a) It is what you know, not necessarily what you have to do about what you know, that succeeds.
- (b) If you make fifty phone calls you will average about 10 per cent success.
- (c) Because we are all similar beings it follows that what I can do, you can do.
- (d) When the product is an expensive item it is always good policy to open on a minor point.
- (e) Whenever you meet an obstacle you should try to turn it

into a stepping stone.

V 2 It takes nearly 100 per cent of a locomotive's power to start a train moving but only about 10 per cent to keep it going. This relates to:

(a) The fact that it takes a lot of effort to get started with phone calls but far less effort to keep on phoning other prospects.

(b) The effort required to lift the receiver is about ten times as great as the effort to speak.

(c) One-tenth of everything we do is likely to result in success.

(d) Much more energy is required to move an object from rest than is required to keep it moving. Getting started is easy, keeping moving becomes progressively more difficult, as there is no longer the same kind of impetus.

(e) The effort of overcoming inertia and procrastination is considerable but, once started on phone calls, it becomes easier.

V 3 Positive thinking is best described as:

(a) The ability to latch on to one set of beliefs while not ignoring any other possibility.

(b) A simple, yet powerful method of concentrating our minds.

(c) Never dwelling on 'losses' of orders, opportunities which have never been possessed.

(d) Looking for good everywhere.

(e) Suppressing negative thoughts about incidents, situations and occurrences, and looking for possible 'plus' points.

V 4 When describing the 'cost of ownership' to a prospect on the phone:

(a) The prospect will learn the real cost of owning a product which may not be priced with its minimum essential accessories.

(b) It is necessary to use a full sales presentation.

(c) The prospect will appreciate running and maintenance costs and depreciation as well as initial purchase.

(d) The benefits of the product should then be listed.

(e) You must listen to make sure that all the salient figures are understood otherwise you may have to try for an appointment close.

V 5 Which of the following do you think would be good telephone openings?

(a) Good morning, Mrs Prospect, my name is Mr Jones. I represent the Smart Homes Decor Service. Do you know that 95 per cent of our customers use us repeatedly every year?

(b) Good morning, Mrs Prospect, my name is Clifford Jones of the Smart Homes Decor Service. Ninety-five per cent of our customers come back to us every year because we do such a good job.

(c) Good morning, Mrs Prospect. My name is Jones of Smart Homes Decor Service. Home decoration, spring cleaning is something we all like to get over quickly. Could you allow me just a few minutes to tell you about our service please?

(d) Good morning, Mrs Prospect, my name is Cliff Jones. I specialize in a complete house decoration service. Our office is in High Street and you can find us in the phone book. Tell me, Mrs Prospect, do you really look forward to house decorating?

(e) Good morning, Mrs Prospect, my name is Jones. I am with the Smart Homes Decor Service. I selected your name from the telephone book. I hope you don't mind. May I tell you about our complete home decoration service?

Block W

W 1 With which of the following statements about telesales openings would you disagree?

(a) Every opening must be a true statement or question, be relevant to the buyer about some specific topic, easily understandable and must evoke interest.

(b) Opening with a question to the prospect implies that the prospect will not be able to answer it readily.

(c) If you open with a specific topic it is essential that you have been in contact with the prospect on some relevant matter previously.

(d) Opening with a question is probably the most useful but, at the same time, the most tricky opening.

(e) If you open using a third party reference it is strongly advisable that the prospect has met the third party.

W 2 You are recommended always to have an objective when you are about to telephone a prospective customer. Which of the following do you consider best defines an objective?

(a) A statement of what is trying to be achieved in a certain

period of time.
(b) A statement of what is to be achieved in terms of the results themselves so that it can be measured.
(c) Where one hopes to be after the telephone call.
(d) What it is expected to be achieved during the phone call.
(e) What you want the prospective customer to do or to agree to.

W 3 Assume that you are telephoning a prospect and you open with a reference to a third party thus: 'Good afternoon, Mr Prospect, this is Bill Wright of Plaster Blocks. I was with John Goodfellow the other day and he suggested I ring you about our latest product.' The prospect replies, 'Who? John Goodfellow? Who's that? Don't know him!' What would you do?
(a) Apologize and ring off as politely as possible then go back to John Goodfellow and check.
(b) Tell him who John Goodfellow is and then ask the prospect if he remembers.
(c) Know that you could not keep the prospect's attention during your sales presentation because he would be thinking all the time, 'Who is John Goodfellow?'
(d) Ignore the question and go straight into your sales presentation and let the prospect know which product the third party is using.
(e) Say 'I'm sorry, Mr Prospect, I seem to have a "crossed wire" somewhere. Anyway, while I'm with you would you mind telling me if your company actually uses items such as plaster blocks?'

W 4 If a prospect raises the question of price during your phone conversation, this is because:
(a) He wishes to buy on price.
(b) He is trying to get some idea of the quality of your product and is using price as the first comparison.
(c) He considers that he may be able to buy a similar product for less.
(d) He does not think that your product is worth what you are asking for it.
(e) You cannot draw any conclusion without more questions.

W 5 It is most important to prepare a sales presentation thoroughly because:
(a) You should be able to go through it like an actor who has learned his part in a play.
(b) Otherwise you will be unable to deal with all the points.

(c) You must control the phone conversation with the prospect.

(d) You must have a degree of flexibility and be able to talk about different aspects of your product if the prospect raises specific questions.

(e) Otherwise you are unable to move naturally to the close.

Block X

X 1 You have made several unsuccessful phone calls and have opened another phone presentation, introduced yourself, the company and the product and the prospective buyer says, 'I'm sorry but I don't know who you are or what you want. What is it you're trying to sell me?' What would you do?

(a) Say, 'Mr Prospect, I'm not trying to sell you anything. I'm hoping to help you buy something. Something that can perhaps, improve your sales.'

(b) Repeat your name, company, and the product you are selling.

(c) Say, 'Mr Prospect, I'm trying to interest you in a –. May I tell you about it now?'

(d) Apologize, replace the receiver and make a note to call again when you have improved your opening.

(e) Apologize and go for a close on an appointment.

X 2 Which of the following are suggested in the book?

(a) Always have at least one specific objective prior to making the phone call.

(b) It is better to make phone calls after lunch.

(c) Every time you receive data from an open probe, try to narrow down the possibilities with closed questions.

(d) Make a brief note of the responses you get to openings so that you can appraise the openings periodically.

(e) As long as you listen carefully to a respondent, it is not necessary to make notes.

X 3 From your reading and understanding about proof statements, these are:

(a) Used only if absolutely necessary during the sales presentation

(b) Generally, used if the prospect finds that your ordinary descriptions are not readily acceptable.

(c) Carefully constructed before the telesales interview and positively demonstrate that your product is worth the asking price.

(d) Carefully constructed before the telesales interview to

convince the prospect of the value of your product.

(e)   Descriptions about the materials, manufacture, experience of usage or performance of the product to prove the quality.

X 4   During your telesales presentation you have identified a need that your prospect has for one of your products. What two things would you do next?

(a)   Restate the need and link it to a product benefit.

(b)   State the need so that the prospect understands it.

(c)   Make sure that the prospect agrees the real nature of his need.

(d)   Attempt to close the sale.

(e)   Make the prospect an offer.

X 5   When selling on the phone:

(a)   The mnemonics AIDA, POWER, TRUE, and ONROAD can be used to develop the sales presentation.

(b)   The opening of the sales presentation should, if possible, involve and interest the respondent.

(c)   You approach the subject of your sales presentation in a similar manner and with the same constraints as a guest speaker at a social occasion.

(d)   If the respondent raises objections early in the conversation you can assume that she or he is interested in your proposition.

(e)   Barriers to buying can be constructed by listening carefully to the respondent and improve your chance of closing the sale.

Block Y

Y 1   Mr Peters deliberates about his ad for a secretary and decides to place a 6 centimetre by two column ad four times in Joan Black's newspaper. If he is satisfied after three insertions, how much will the ads cost?

(a)   £384.

(b)   £288.

(c)   £216.

(d)   £192.

(e)   £108.

Y 2   It is essential when you make an offer on the phone:

(a)   That it relates to thé benefits of the product and not just its features or attributes.

(b)   That it follows your statement of the prospect's need.

(c)   That the price is stated clearly in terms that the prospect understands, that is, if he is buying in cases of 12, you do not quote the bottle price, or if he uses metric tonnes, you do not quote in tons.

(d) You either explicitly state or clearly imply the time limit for which the offer is open.

(e) It relates to the real needs of the prospective customer.

Y 3 Two 'tried and proven' methods of closing sales are mentioned in the book. They are:

(a) Tell the prospect that the price will be increased by about 10 per cent for the next consignment.

(b) The alternative close.

(c) Letting the prospect know that there are very few of the products left: the 'last few' close.

(d) Getting the prospect to say 'yes' all the time by appropriate questions.

(e) The 'leave the door open' close.

Y 4 With which of the following statements do you agree are possible in a telephone sales presentation but are not necessarily discussed in the book?

(a) Phone calls are expensive, therefore try to close as quickly as possible.

(b) It is not good sales presentation to have to ask for the order.

(c) Don't be in a hurry to get off the phone if you have secured the order or appointment because it is rather rude.

(d) Whenever you hear a 'buying signal' always attempt a close.

(e) It is normally possible to be a little more direct on the phone when closing.

Y 5 According to the discussion in the book, you may interpret the saying, 'keep your powder dry' to mean:

(a) Do not give too much information too soon.

(b) Avoid getting into a situation where you have to sell on the phone when you really should wait until the normal face-to-face selling situation.

(c) Shoot your main selling points when it suits you rather than in an off-hand manner.

(d) Secrete your selling points at all times.

(e) If you tell little bits of your sales story here and there, it will erode your overall presentation and weaken your chances of success.

Block Z

Z 1 With which of the following do you think the author of the book would disagree?
  (a) Always make suitable selections of prospects you propose to phone.
  (b) Don't be afraid of using long, descriptive words.
  (c) Once you have decided on the objective for your phone call, it is not good practice to change it.
  (d) Some products and services can only normally be sold at a personal face-to-face interview so avoid satisfying requests for further information over the phone and concentrate on closing for an appointment.
  (e) If you are seeking to close an appointment and the prospect says that he is too busy, you are damaging your chances of success if you persist in trying to close an appointment.

Z 2 From your reading and understanding of the book and your general knowledge of business, which of the following are correct?
  (a) The real cost of ownership relates to the return achieved from the investment in the product.
  (b) The cost of ownership is the increased cost of using the product.
  (c) Assessment of a proposition can be in financial or non-financial terms.
  (d) If you are working on a profit of 15 per cent and give the buyer an extra 5 per cent discount, your profit is reduced to 10 per cent.
  (e) If you are working on a profit of 15 per cent and give the buyer an extra 5 per cent discount, your profit is reduced by $33\frac{1}{3}$ per cent.

Z 3 With which of the following do you agree?
  (a) What is important is not so much the extra discount you are forced to give to a buyer but by how much your profit is reduced. Giving away another 5 per cent discount on a transaction where you normally make 20 per cent profit means that your profit has been reduced by 25 per cent.
  (b) If your profit is reduced by 25 per cent, you need to sell an additional $33\frac{1}{3}$ per cent volume to compensate.
  (c) If your profit is reduced by 20 per cent you need to sell an additional 25 per cent volume to compensate.
  (d) If you usually give 20 per cent discount and the prospect insists on the phone that he needs another 5 per cent say,

'All right less 20 less another 5,' because this is less than giving less 25 per cent.

(e) It is no use preparing lots of possible percentage discounts because you do not know what the prospect is likely to ask on the phone.

Z 4 With which of the following do you consider that the author of this book would disagree?

(a) Whenever you pick up the phone to make or take a call make sure you have something to write with and something to write on.

(b) Don't read through the whole book, or even a whole chapter before you practise techniques and skills you read about in this book.

(c) If you intend to improve your telephone selling technique, you should study all the chapters and relevant exercises in the book before you attempt to apply some of the principles in practice.

(d) The important selling sentences in your presentation should be reviewed and revised from time to time so as to keep them up-to-date.

(e) If you use open probes and closed questions carefully when selling on the telephone, you will always be able to establish the real needs of a prospective customer before you make the offer.

Z 5 Which of the following are intimated or stated in the book?

(a) Positive thinking is continually adapting your thoughts to a changing world and searching for plus points.

(b) Opening a telephone sale on a specific topic should have the same qualities of truth, relevance, understanding and interest as opening with a factual statement.

(c) It is essential always to control the phone conversation and not to let questions from the prospect divert you from your preplanned presentation.

(d) Never make an offer until the prospect has agreed his need with you.

(e) Perhaps the most useful advice to the telesales person is to listen carefully to all responses made by the prospective customer.

Objectivity test answers

Block U			
1	a b	d	
2			e
3	b		
4	b	d	
5	None		

Block V		
1		e
2	a	e
3		e
4	c	
5	c	

Block W			
1	a b c		e
2	b		
3			e
4			e
5		d	

Block X			
1		c	
2	a		d
3			e
4	b c		
5	b		

Block Y			
1	b		
2			e
3	None		
4		d	e
5	a b c		e

Block Z			
1		c	e
2		c d	e
3	a b	d	
4		c	c
5	a b		e

Index